OWLS
Their Life and Behavior

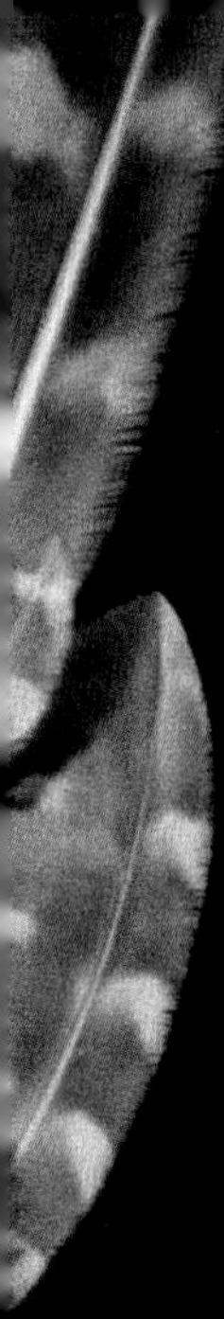

A PHOTOGRAPHIC

STUDY OF

THE NORTH AMERICAN

SPECIES

OWLS

Their Life and

Behavior

Text by Julio de la Torre

PHOTOGRAPHS BY ART WOLFE

Foreword by Roger Tory Peterson

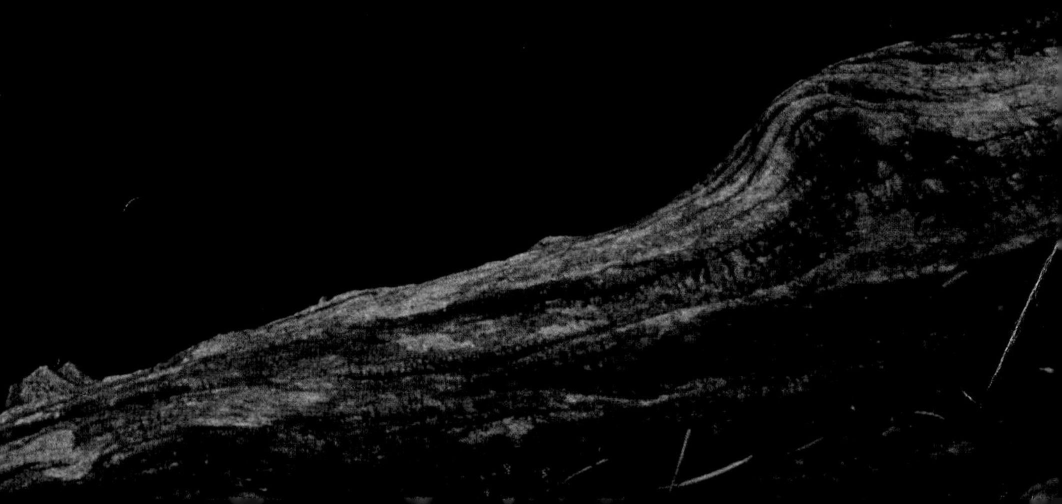

Crown Publishers, Inc., New York

Copyright © 1990 by Julio de la Torre
Photographs copyright © 1990 by Art Wolfe

Published by Crown Publishers, Inc., 201 East 50th Street, New York, New York 10022

CROWN is a trademark of Crown Publishers, Inc.

Manufactured in Japan

Library of Congress Cataloging-in-Publication Data

de la Torre, Julio, 1934–
    Owls : their life and behavior.
    Bibliography: p.
    Includes index.
    1. Owls—North America.   I. Title.
QL696.S8D4   1989   598'.97'097   89-7894

ISBN 0-517-57488-8

Design by Lauren Dong
Illustrations by Annemarie Sandstrom

10 9 8 7 6 5 4 3 2 1

First Edition

The photographs on pages i, ii–iii, and x show, respectively, a juvenile long-eared owl in flight; an adult spotted owl lighting on a tree branch; and a spotted owl in a quiet perch amid vine maples in an old-growth forest in Oregon's Cascade Mountains.

To the memory of Robert S. Arbib, Jr.

CONTENTS

Left to right: A saw-whet owl, a juvenile great horned owl, a barred owlet showing the beautiful blue eye-color of some immature owls, and an adult screech owl.

ACKNOWLEDGMENTS

For students of bird life, owls are the last frontier. Researchers continually sally forth into forest and field armed with telemetry devices, night vision scopes, boom boxes, and the ardor of adventure, seeking to unveil the secrets of this most mysterious of bird families.

The volume of work done on owls is enormous. A bibliography of titles in English fills a tome twice as thick as this one. A comprehensive monograph would probably crush the reader with its weight, if not indeed its cost. Our aim has been less ambitious and more practical: a pictorial study of the North American owl species, with up-to-date biological data, summaries of natural history, surveys of anatomy and behavior, and hints on how to find owls in the field.

Even with its modest scale, our book could never have been written without the help of many individuals. At the American Museum of Natural History, New York City, Dean Amadon and John Bull gave support and advice and Allison Andors provided unstinting assistance. Special thanks are due to Eleanor Stickney, curator at the Peabody Museum of Natural History, Yale University, for the loan of specimen materials used in the technical drawings. John Ostrom read the chapter on fossil owls and made helpful suggestions. Dwight Smith was a treasure chest of information, in addition to helping in the field. Richard Clark answered questions about hawk owls. Joe T. Marshall, Jr., cleared up difficult points in the classification of screech owls. Charles Sibley shed light on owl systematics in general. Paul Kerlinger made available material on snowy owls and on owl migrations. Gordon Dee Alcorn provided specimens and advice. Andrea Priori, of the Cornell Laboratory of Ornithology, supplied tapes of rare owl calls. John K. Terres, in a lavish gesture, made available close to fifty years' worth of research on the owls; our gratitude to him transcends words.

Words also fail when trying to thank Russ and Jane Kinne for their unsparing generosity. Art wishes to express his gratitude to the many field biologists who helped him locate owls over the years. Without their assistance the project might never have been completed. Especially generous were the contributions of Susanna Goad, Greg Green, Dr. Richard Reynolds, Ralph Anderson, Ron Ryder, Mark Henjum, Greg and Pat Hayward, Ed Garton, and Eric Forsman. Julio owes a special debt to Joe Zeranski and Bob Boone, "inventors" of the owl prowl, as well as to Tom Burke, Fred Purnell, Tom Baptist, Steve Faccio, and John Schull, boon companions of many a moonlit foray.

Max Gartenberg's princely presence pervades the entire book; he truly was the sine qua non. To Brandt Aymar, our editor at Crown, thanks for exemplary patience and for steering the manuscript through the inevitable reefs and shoals. The beauty of the book is largely due to the genius of Lauren Dong, our marvelous designer. All of these people contributed to the merits of our book; the flaws, if any, are ours.

FOREWORD

What is there about owls that fascinates humans as well as the small birds that mob them? Totally different reasons, of course. Do we see a reflection of ourselves in the forward-facing eyes that seem framed in outsized spectacles, giving the birds a professorial look? (Actually, the "silly goose" may have more smarts than the "wise old owl," but we cannot be sure.) Owls are what they are, and they are very good at it.

The anthropomorphic view of owls may account for their popularity as figurines and other collectibles, exceeded among birds only by the popularity of penguins—which, again, reflect the human animal: Penguins stand erect with flippers at their sides, just as we do.

There have been other books about owls; I have a full shelf of them, most of them illustrated with drawings or paintings. However, no other book has offered such a superb collection of photographs of all our North American species, taken by a master of the most advanced photographic techniques: Art Wolfe. Not a "point-and-shoot" photographer, Art Wolfe knows how to make the most sophisticated equipment behave. I am impressed. I have walked the nocturnal woods with owl prowlers near my home in Connecticut and elsewhere—even as far away as Botswana, where I photographed Pel's fishing owl while hippos and crocodiles threatened. So I know what has gone into this book.

Only a few birds of the night other than owls elicit a similar sort of fascination—the whippoorwills and their relatives, perhaps; some of the rails; and a few others. When we explore the dark aisles of the woodlands or mysterious riverine areas, we use our senses to full capacity, especially our sight and our hearing.

In these well-researched and well-written pages, Julio de la Torre, an inveterate owl prowler, tells us all about these nocturnal birds and their mythology, as well as the love-hate relationship and superstitions that they have inspired in people down through the ages. We then go on to learn more about their classification, evaluation, biology, behavior, ecology, and conservation. Thanks to the lively prose and sound scholarship of Julio de la Torre, I now know a lot more about our North American owls than I did.

ROGER TORY PETERSON

OWLS
*Their Life and
Behavior*

THE OWL

Left: A saw-whet owl prepares to leave the nesting cavity after having fed its young. Right: Three great horned owlets perch in a ponderosa pine, an example of branching behavior.

L ong before the age of recorded history people carved owls in ivory, crawled into lightless caves to etch their likeness on walls with sharpened bones, and painted them with vegetable dyes on steep canyon walls. For owls are fascinating birds. From the dainty saw-whet owl, looking out curiously from the depths of a spruce, to the awesome great horned owl, gliding silently in the twilight, they have long impressed us with their mysterious ways, delighted our eye with the beauty of their billowing plumage, and excited our imagination with their hypnotic eyes—huge, brilliant, forever seeming to penetrate the secrets of nature.

As bird groups go, the owl family is not especially large, numbering about 160 species. But what grand birds it contains! To name just three, the burrowing owl has long been a tourist attraction in Florida; the Owl of Athena was credited with helping the Greeks win the Battle of Marathon;

and the barn owl, champion flying mousetrap, is a probable origin of the idea of ghosts.

Owls have been called cats with wings—an excellent analogy. Like cats, owls are admirably fitted for hunting in the dark. Both are sleek, powerful predators, with bewitching eyes that seem to glow in the dark but that are in fact marvelous optical instruments able to adjust in an instant from telescope to microscope, with a pupil that responds in fractions of a second to the most minute changes in light intensity.

The ears of owls, like those of cats, are exceptionally keen. Some owls are able to catch mice in total darkness simply by zeroing in on the patter of their tiny feet, barely audible to our ears. Owl talons are much like cat claws—razor sharp and very mobile, with great gripping power. A great horned owl can easily snap the neck of a large woodchuck. And, finally, when it comes to courting, the behavior of cats and owls is remarkably similar. The self-respecting owl loves nothing quite so much as shattering the silence of a moonlit night with a cacophony of hoots, moans, and caterwauls in pursuit of romance.

To all of these features, the owl adds a special one: silent, or near-silent, flight. Few things in nature surprise one more than the sight of a great gray owl unfurling its gigantic wings—its wingspread can be close to six feet—to flap away with no more noise than a downy plume makes floating in the breeze.

Owls and cats haven't just "gone to sea in a beautiful pea-green boat"; they have ridden together the tides of history and religion, enjoying moments of glory, then sinking to the lowest depths of disrepute. Owls in particular have been variously loved as cute and comical, worshipped as idols, and loathed as reincarnations of the devil. Their features appear on bronze vases from ancient China, Egyptian bas-reliefs, Athenian coins, Persian miniatures, and pre-Columbian talismans. Renaissance silverware, French porcelain, and Victorian bibelots abound with owls. Probably no other group of birds, except perhaps the penguin, has been used so often to amuse the human animal. Both birds resemble us in such a way that we just cannot resist reading our foibles into their features.

Unlike penguins, however, owls have been linked to humans in intimate and perturbing ways since our earliest ancestors roamed the earth. Owls love eating rodents; where people live, rodents flourish. Owls choose caves and sheltered ledges for nesting and roosting; both, of course, have always been choice spots

for the campsites and permanent dwellings of primitive, and not so primitive, tribes, from prehistoric times to the present day. A family of snowy owls etched on the wall of an Ice Age cave at Trois Frères, France, and the Owl-Man depicted by Stone Age aborigines on the rock wall of another cave in Balu-Uru, Australia, halfway around the world, prove both the universality of home sharing and the grip that owls had on the mind of early man. For

these human ancestors three million years ago, as for us today, the booming hoots, tremulous wailings, and hair-raising shrieks of creatures we rarely see have been cause for wonder and terror; when seen, their erect posture and fixed, humanoid stare have been a source of fascination. Above all, the owls' uncanny ability to materialize suddenly and silently out of the dark has conspired with their other qualities to surround them with a truly archetypal aura of mystery.

It is hardly surprising, then, that we have woven the owl into the tapestry of our legends, literature, and art. Here indeed are Ovid's monsters of the night—the Striges—feathered witches that snatched babies from the cradle. Here too is the emblem of wisdom, the imperturbable, penetrating, far-sighted Owl of Athena, proudly perched on the shoulders of that great Olympic goddess.

A spotted owl in flight prepares to attack prey.

OWL FOLKLORE
A Sampler

Left: A great horned owl perches on a tree stump. Hunting activity often commences in the early evening. Right: Five barn owlets in various stages of development at their nesting site in a barn.

*L*et Pallas Athena, the owl-eyed daughter of Zeus, lead us into the owl's mythic past. She, to many the most appealing of the Olympians, was worshipped by the Hellenic Greeks, those most appealing pagans. The Greeks, who gave us the concept of an order of nature, treated the owl with appreciation and humor.

Athene noctua, *the little owl, was their mascot. Guardian of the Acropolis, the little owl not only peered wisely at the world from the obverse of Athenian coins but accompanied Greek armies to battle. Aristophanes attributed the victory at Marathon to a flock of hissing owls that swooped down on the Persian foe, sowing terror and confusion through the ranks.*

Almost two centuries later, when the glory of Greece was fading and Rome's splendor had not yet attained its zenith, another general claimed that owls had helped him win a great victory over the Carthaginians—Agathocles,

Tyrant of Syracuse, an ally of Rome but still a Greek.

In stark contrast with the lucid spirit of Greece, the Roman mind saw omens in everything; obscurantism mushroomed like mildew in a damp cellar. Here is where ornithomancy—ceremonial divination from birds—rose to an exalted place in the state religion, with augurs ("bird talk" experts, who listened to what the birds said) and auspices ("bird watchers," who tried to read the future in bird entrails) as high priests. Julius Caesar was a respected augur. What happened to the hero birds of Marathon in the hands of this gang of glorified soothsayers?

First the Greek gods had been brought over, drained of life, and renamed. Athena became Minerva and was allowed to keep her owl. The mascot of Mount Olympus now reigned over the Palatine Hill. But in her new setting the poor owl became an omen of disaster. Her reign was a reign of terror.

All of the fears that owls engendered among primitive tribes—who endowed them with mysterious powers; created rituals to propitiate them and incantations to exorcise them; and devised icons, totems, and talismans to trap their magic and make it their own—gathered to a head in Rome and were made respectable in the words of Augustan authors. Ovid, in particular, takes his discussion of owls to an extreme. In *Fasti,* he says the owl was called a "screechwitch" (*strix*) because of its habit of screeching "stridently" (*stridere*) through the night. But Ovid also insists that striges eat babies. And, as if that were not enough, he says they also smell bad!

For the flimflam about owls as messengers of death, bearers of ill tidings, and omens of doom, our source is no less than Pliny the Elder. In Book X of his *Natural History*—an amazing potpourri of facts and fantasy that was, nevertheless, respected in its day and remained a standard reference work through the Renaissance—he wrote that the owl

> ". . . is the very monster of the night . . . when it appears it foretells nothing but evil . . . if it be seen within cities, or otherwise abroad in any place, it is not for good, but prognosticates some fearful misfortune."

Pliny actually reflects an older, well-established tradition. In the Old Testament, for instance, owls are anathemized as unclean, often appearing together with vultures and jackals in scenes of pestilence and desolation or enhancing the gloom of a devastated village, the cohorts of "dragons and satyrs."

Unfortunately, this tradition, rather than that of the Greeks, dominated in the Middle Ages, when owls and cats were seen as the familiars of witches and warlocks. A different kind of augur began interpreting their wails, still considered to presage death and disaster. Owl feathers, talons, eyes, and droppings made their way into countless concoctions, none likely to gain the approval of the village priest. What a fall from grace was here: to be wrenched from the shoulder of Pallas Athena and placed on that of Beelzebub!

Throughout this long decline, belief in the beneficent side of owls did not die out altogether. The most quaint of these beliefs are embodied in a multitude of customs connecting owls with fertility, many of which are still to be found in what is left of the rural peasantry in Europe, South America, and Asia. Both Sicilians and natives of Provence will recommend that a young man take an uncooperative lady to a cottage ascertained to harbor a hooting owl; amorous conquest is then assured.

In localities in Wales and the south of France it is believed that an owl shrieking in the vicinity of a pregnant woman means an easy delivery or the birth of a baby girl, or both. Could this be sympathetic white magic, the cries of the mother in labor being prefigured, and eased, by the doleful wail of the owl? Could the link between owls, women, and pregnancy be bound up in the fact that so many owls look like fat babies, if not indeed like pregnant Toby jugs?

Related to the above is the ancient theme of lunacy. In his delightful book *The Nightwatchers* Angus Cameron reveals the tie between owls, the moon, and man. The cycles of sexual ardor, both human and strixine, coincide with, if they are not indeed, as some have stated, triggered by, lunar cycles. The moon, it seems, arouses both owls and people.

John Sparks tells us that in India owl meat is supposed to be an aphrodisiac. On the other hand, if you eagerly attack a bowl of owl ragout in hopes of reanimating a collapsed libido you run the risk of becoming a fool and losing your memory.

The use of owls as amulets and talismans among so-called primitive peoples, from Cro-Magnon cavemen to the Aztecs of Mexico to the present-day Pueblo Indians of the southwest, and their almost universal integration into tribal rituals connected with ancestor worship and the burial of the dead is not only matched but probably surpassed by the extensive and diversified employment of these birds in therapeutic applications. The restorative and remedial powers of owls span the spectrum of human imaginings, from Persian remedies for palsy (rub affected area with warm owl blood), wasp infestations (burn owl dung in the fireplace), and migraine (mix owl marrow with oil of violets for nose drops); to an old Roman nostrum for snakebite (plumbago herb mixed with burnt owls' feet, cited by Pliny); to Cyranides's cure for epilepsy ("soup made from owls' eggs, while the moon was waning," per John Sparks); to cures for head lice, hives, whooping cough, incontinence, and insomnia.

Two odd beliefs deserve special note. One is the use of owls to extract secrets. The trick is to place an owl, or part of an owl, on a sleeping person whose secrets one wants to discover. Roman matrons were thus obliged to disclose clandestine affairs. Though Pliny thought the idea a fraud, it retained its currency down through the ages, surfacing in 1819 among the Amish of Reading, Pennsylvania, in a German-language book titled *The Long Hidden Friend*, where the following advice was given: "If you lay the heart and right foot of a Barn Owl on one who is asleep, he will answer whatever you ask him, and tell what he has done."

This sober counsel brings us to the second theme: drunkenness. Widespread throughout the Mediterranean basin is the belief that owls' eggs are an effective nostrum against intemperance. What is again remarkable here is the duration and tenacity of the idea. From ancient times to the present, in many different cultural contexts, the eggs of owls have been venerated as agencies of abstemiousness.

Finally, there is the connection between owls and ghosts, a closer one than most people think. I am convinced that *Tyto alba*, the common barn owl, is no less than the original Halloween spook. Barn owls and men have lived together for three million years. Often these owls will punctuate otherwise silent glides with bone-chilling shrieks. These loud, raspy sounds are just the thing to unhinge the mind of an unsuspecting stroller in the night wood. Barn owls also have a call that sounds a good deal like pieces of metal clicking together. Uttered mostly in or close to their roosts, this call could easily be mistaken for the sound of chains being dragged by a specter.

Barn owls are shaped like the "schmoos" of Al Capp's immortal *Li'l Abner*. They look entirely white from below. Their dark eyes appear to be jet black. Now and then they pick up bioluminescent fungi and therefore seem to glow in the dark. Add to this the barn owl's habit of haunting ancient ruins, abandoned cemeteries, crumbling belfries, and decaying farmhouses—not forgetting that fear can magnify objects—and you will have no difficulty in visualizing the archetype of the ectoplasmic spirit.

What then is a haunted house? A dilapidated structure inhabited by barn owls! The locale might be a suburban brownstone or a battered antebellum mansion—it matters little. Decay, rattling noises, and weird white shapes whooshing by, glowing in the dark, are age-old elements of the classic horror yarn.

With the advent of the Renaissance and the Enlightenment, natural science came into its own, and with it the fog of superstition enshrouding owls lifted . . . at least in educated circles. Bizarre beliefs still remain. Let them go on, as long as they do no harm to the owl or the believer. Owls are an inexhaustible source of fascination, and the facts about them are no less interesting than the legends.

CLASSIFICATION OF OWLS

Left: A flammulated owl delivers prey (a grub) to young in their nest cavity. Right: A hunting spotted owl.

*T*axonomists today classify the owl tribe in the order Strigiformes, between the cuckoos (order Cuculiformes) and the nightjars, frogmouths, oilbirds, and potoos (order Caprimulgiformes). Nightjars include such familiar birds as the whippoorwill and the bullbat, or common nighthawk. The owls' kinship to this group is more truly evident at the molecular level—as revealed in egg protein analysis and more recently through the technique of DNA-DNA hybridization developed by Professors Charles Sibley and Jon Ahlquist—than in parallel adaptations to a life of hunting in the dark, which could be the result of evolutionary convergence.

Convergence is what occurs when in the course of evolution two groups of animals that exploit the same niche, but are not closely related, wind up looking like each other through the development of similar adaptations. Convergence is at the root of the equipment that owls have in common with falcons and hawks. These shared traits are so dramatic that the two groups were once thought to be phylogenetically akin. Like many scientific ideas, this one has been discarded, revived, and revamped at various times. The consensus today is that owls and hawks are convergent—they look alike because both groups have evolved the tools that a flying hunter needs to survive.

According to the checklist followed in this work (Amadon & Bull), the order of owls numbers 164 species in one family, the Strigidae, which has two subfamilies. The first of these, the Tytoninae, comprises eleven species of barn and grass owls (genus *Tyto*) and two species of bay owls (genus *Phodilus*). The other subfamily, the Striginae, or so-called typical owls, comprises the remaining species. Until recently, the barn, grass, and bay owls were assigned full family rank, but much controversy surrounded the idea of separating the *Tyto* owls in a category that would place them in a relationship to other owls like that of bobcats to foxes, or foxes to weasels. Anatomical and behavioral differences, in the light of demonstrable relatedness at the molecular level, suddenly do not appear very significant. We have, moreover, proof at a far more dramatic and visible level. A captive barn owl was hybridized with a striped owl (*Asio clamator*), a typical strigid species, and produced fertile eggs, thus bringing down a bastion of traditional taxonomy.

EVOLUTION
The Story of the Oldest Owls

O *wls have been around a long time.*
DNA hybridization data take us
back to the Cretaceous Period, eighty million years ago, to the fork in the
evolutionary road where owls and nightjars went their separate ways. These
two great orders of nocturnal predators are generally acknowledged to be
descended from a common ancestor. What this forebear looked like no one
knows. For that matter it isn't easy to say what the oldest creatures supposed
to have been owls were like. Based on Upper Cretaceous fossils from Romania,
a family of owls, the Bradycnemidae, was described in 1975 by C.J.O.
Harrison and C. A. Walker, but their conclusions have been challenged by
David Steadman.* Another expert, Alan Feduccia, says these owls were small
dinosaurs. The full name of Harrison and Walker's presumptive owl, quar-
ried as it was from Transylvanian limestone, is Bradycneme draculae.

Though it may be interesting to speculate about a dinosaur-owl that
returns to its coffin at dawn, such a bird remains a questionable hybrid.
There is, however, no question about its antiquity or that of several related
forms, which undoubtedly included the true ancestral owls. These creatures
hunted in cycad forests during a period when giant dinosaurs still ruled the
earth. It is not too farfetched to visualize an ancestor of our dainty saw-whet
owl chomping on an outsize dragonfly a few feet away from a delta-dwelling
hadrosaur, with a triceratops and maybe even a fearsome tyrannosaur look-
ing on from high ground.

The "monster lizards" were not to last much longer, however. As every

---

* *See under* Owl Pellets, Chapter 7, for reference to Steadman's work on fossil faunas.

GEOLOGICAL TIME SCALE

Era	Period	Epoch	MYA*	Owls and Other Birds	Other Life
CENOZOIC *(age of birds and mammals)*	QUATERNARY	Recent	0.01	All owl groups reach peak *Ornimegalonyx;* giant sloths	Man
		Pleistocene	1.5–3.5		
	TERTIARY	Pliocene	7	*Aegolius*(?) *Surnia*(?) Tytonids and strigids expand *Bubo, Otus, Strix* Tytonid owls Quercy fauna *Eostrix, Minerva* *Ogygoptynx* (first owl)	Rats and mice
		Miocene	26		Hominids
		Oligocene	37–38		Voles
		Eocene	53–54		Rodents
		Paleocene	65		Seed-bearing plants
MESOZOIC *(age of dinosaurs)*	CRETACEOUS	Late	100	Strigiformes (owls) Caprimulgiformes (nightjars) Common ancestor	Last of the dinosaurs
		Early	135		
	JURASSIC	Late	155	*Archeopteryx* (first recognized bird) 175 MYA	Dinosaurs rule undisputed over planet
		Middle	170		
		Early	180–190		Dinosaurs flourish
	TRIASSIC		230	*Protoavis* (hypothetical first bird)	Early dinosaurs

* MYA = million years ago

schoolboy knows, some sort of cataclysm occurred at the end of the Cretaceous Period that caused the extinction of these magnificent animals, an incredibly diversified group that had been the undisputed lords of land, water, and air for more than 150 million years. The precise nature of the catastrophe is a controversial topic that has been exhaustively explored in many recent books.

For our purposes, the key point to be made is that the dividing line between the Cretaceous Period and the Tertiary is sharp and dramatic. Called the K/T Boundary, it can be discerned in many places where Tertiary rocks overlay Cretaceous layers. Many reptiles crossed the K/T Boundary unscathed, including a few dinosaurs. The birds did, too. And so did an odd group of fuzzy little creatures with long snouts and nasty dispositions, whose progeny was destined to inherit the planet. These, of course, were the myria smallish and then seemingly inconsequential early mammals.

It was at the dawn of this new period that

the oldest bird so far accepted as a genuine owl made its appearance. It chose to do so in Colorado, a habitat probably warmer and wetter than, but otherwise very likely resembling, the semiopen foothill country of today. There were, however, few flowering plants and apparently no rodents—most significant from an owl's point of view.

In 1916 a pocket of rock about the size of a kitchen cabinet was quarried near Tiffany, Colorado. Probably the petrified remains of a carnivore's den, the pocket was full of bones that date back sixty million years. This places the bones (collectively known as the Tiffanian Fauna) in the Paleocene Epoch, which immediately followed the Cretaceous Period. Among the gems in this cache was the tarsometatarsus (upper foot and ankle) of a bird of prey. Alexander Wetmore, one of America's most prolific ornithologists, originally identified it as belonging to an eagle. Subsequently, Wetmore examined similar leg bones dating from the Eocene Epoch, fifteen million years later than the Tiffanian discovery. Declaring these bones to be owl bones, he gave the birds that had possessed them the generic name *Protostrix* (first owl). For many years thereafter protostrigid owls were regarded as the oldest known members of the Flying Mousetrap Club. Then the Tiffanian tarsometatarsus was redescribed by Pat Rich and David Bohaska, who concluded that this ankle/foot belonged not to an eagle but to an owl. Everyone agreed. Rebaptized *Ogygoptynx wetmorei*,* the prehistoric Coloradan is now accepted as the first undoubted owl.

Ogygoptynx was not only older but quite different from *Protostrix*. The latter was obviously a bird that seized and killed mammals. *Ogygoptynx*, on the other hand, probably thrived chiefly on arthropods.

This difference becomes clear through a comparison of the tarsometatarsi. The protostrigid foot/ankle is impressive. The specimen illustrated on page 16, though shortish, is thick and has massive trochleae—the pulley-like structures on which the tendons that retract the claws glide. These were obviously the frame for the powerful flexors and extensors needed to snap the neck of a mid-Eocene opossum. In contrast, the ankle/foot of *Ogygoptynx* is slender and elegant. Its trochleae are less massive and protuberant. In birds of prey this kind of structure is associated with talons that are long and feathery, propelled by pliant and flexible flexors, allied with longish, usually

unfeathered legs, anatomical features enabling their possessor to stalk through open country feeding on scorpions, locusts, beetles, and the myriad other crunchy delicacies provided by the Arthropoda—that most bountiful of all animal groups.

Living raptors with life-styles like that suggested for *Ogygoptynx* are the secretary bird of Africa, the crested caracara (the national bird of Mexico), and—most significantly—the burrowing owl. It would not be altogether absurd to speculate that the Tiffanian foot might have belonged to a bird that looked like a burrowing owl. Placing the *Ogygoptynx* foot side by side with that of a "billy owl" can be a revelation. On page 16 the tarsometatarsi of both birds are drawn to scale along with those of *Protostrix* and several extant owls. Imaginary flesh and claws have been added to the fossil bones.

The similarity between the ankle/foot of the fossil raptor and that of the burrowing owl is certainly suggestive. One might easily believe that the first "accepted" owl was none other than the ancestor of this well-known and much loved species, quite alive today and carrying out its appointed rounds not far from where the bones of its prehistoric forebear were exhumed in 1916. However, the fact that the feet of both species look alike does not necessarily mean that the birds were identical; convergent evolution can play subtle tricks. Nonetheless, there is nothing implausible about extrapolating look-alike owls from similar leg bones.

Buttressing the argument that the earliest owl may have run about on long, lightly feathered legs, hunting for insects in open country, is the fact that rodents do not seem to have been a component of the Tiffanian Fauna. Not long afterward they did swarm over the American West, having apparently crossed over from Asia on an early Bering Strait land bridge. Here it is important to clarify the relationship between rodents and burrowing owls. Billy owls *do* catch and eat small rodents, including an occasional baby prairie dog. However, they kill this kind of prey by severing the spinal cord with their beaks. Their talons can grab a mouse but are not strong enough to finish it off.

Returning to the Paleocene, we can easily imagine *Ogygoptynx* as closely resembling a burrowing owl and yet making a perfectly decent living in those antediluvian days. The land teemed with reptiles, including tortoises

---

* From the Greek, *Ogyges,* mythical king of Thebes, suggesting antiquity, and *ptynx,* an owl; *wetmorei* in honor of Alexander Wetmore.

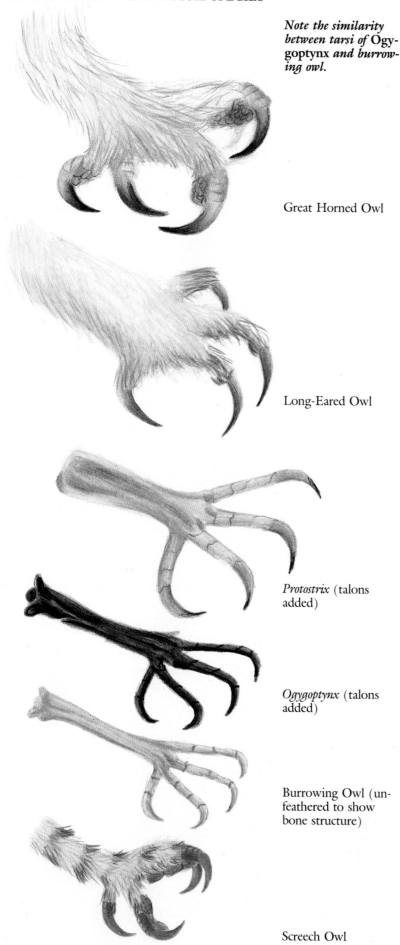

Note the similarity between tarsi of **Ogygoptynx** *and burrowing owl.*

Great Horned Owl

Long-Eared Owl

Protostrix (talons added)

Ogygoptynx (talons added)

Burrowing Owl (unfeathered to show bone structure)

Screech Owl

and a large assortment of lizards, which might have supplied the owl with nesting burrows and an occasional meal. Not to be overlooked as a possible source of cozy holes in the ground are fossorial marsupials, probably too big to eat, but just as acceptable as real estate agents and neighbors as prairie dogs are today. We must also remember that billy owls can and regularly do excavate their own burrows. There is no reason to believe *Ogygoptynx* could not have done so, too. So much for homemaking analogies. What about food? A good retort to the platitude that insects will someday rule the earth is that they have been ruling it for over four hundred million years. Individuals representing almost every form known today may be seen perfectly preserved in pieces of Paleocene amber. So our hypothetical insect-eating owl would have been as content as Falstaff with his endless supply of mead, venison, and roast boar.

The notion that *Ogygoptynx wetmorei* might have been closely related to, if not indeed conspecific with, the burrowing owl has fascinating biological implications. *Athene cunicularia,* the burrowing owl, not only is not primitive but is in fact conceded to be a highly evolved bird. In a comprehensive reclassification of the owls, N. L. Ford places the genera *Athene, Surnia* (the northern hawk owl), and *Aegolius* (the boreal and saw-whet owls) together in an advanced subfamily, the Surniinae.* This implies that Sibley and Ahlquist's date for the separation of owls and nightjars might plausibly be moved back a notch or two, possibly to the end of the Jurassic Period, 135 million years ago. After all, in one of their most remarkable revisions based on DNA-DNA hybridization, the same team concluded that Australian bird families regarded as much later than owls in the evolutionary scale diverged in the Cretaceous Period.

There is little doubt that owls diversified dramatically and spread across the globe during the early to middle Tertiary. This radiation coincides with the rise of a new primary resource, seeds, and of a secondary one, mice and their allies—seed eaters par excellence. The angiosperms, or seed-bearing plants, had put forth experimental models long before the Tertiary, but during the Eocene they diversified explosively. As these flowering plants overwhelmed the araucarians, cycads, cypresses, and ferns that for millions of years had been the dominant terrestrial flora, a mosaic of

---

* For more on the evolutionary relationships of *Surnia* and *Aegolius* see the entry for the northern hawk owl in Chapter 6, the Portfolio section.

new grasslands and forests gradually formed. Closely tracking the flora, the newly evolved families of mammals burst into a kaleidoscope of new forms. A multitude of moles, shrews, and, most significantly, rodents rose to fill the profusion of niches that rapidly became available. For each new resource a new exploiter evolved—hawks and falcons scything the sky by day, owls intently scanning the world at night.

Seven owl species so far are known from the Eocene in North America. Four of these are in the genus *Protostrix* and two in the genus *Eostrix*. One, *Minerva antiqua*, represents a fascinating discovery. The powerful protostrigids (or perhaps more accurately the wise Minervas, as will shortly become apparent) shared the land with remarkable creatures. Among the birds none was more striking than the huge flightless Diatryma. Though not as tall as the elephant birds of Madagascar (source of the Roc in Sinbad the Sailor tales), they were the heaviest birds the world has ever known. Long regarded as fearsome flesh eaters (filling the niche of the extinct carnivorous dinosaurs), Diatrymas have been convincingly recast as harmless herbivores by paleontologist Allison Andors. The mammals of the time included *Titanotherium*, a rhinoceros-like giant, and *Eohippus*, the dainty "dawn horse" that evolved into the Clydesdale.

Those of us who have been seduced by the myth that paleontologists can reconstruct a whole animal from a toenail might now consider the case of *Minerva antiqua*. A Middle Eocene fossil from Tabernacle Butte, Wyoming—now uncontestedly accepted as an owl—was mistaken for an edentate mammal.* The eminent French paleornithologist Cécile Mourer-Chauviré examined the fossil and sensed that something was amiss. Noting that the animal had flexors and extensors like those of any modern owl, she returned the mammal to the birds, and *Minerva* was resurrected as an owl. Further study made it clear to Mourer-Chauviré that her rehabilitated owl and the protostrigids were congeneric and that the name *Protostrix*, clearly a misnomer in view of *Ogygoptynx*, should be dropped in favor of *Minerva*.

With the advent of the Oligocene Epoch a striking development took place. In Quercy, France, a remarkable fossil fauna was found preserved in phosphorite deposits. Among the many birds recovered from Quercy, eleven species in seven genera are owls. The entire assemblage was recently reexamined by Mourer-Chauviré and determined to belong, almost en bloc, to the Tytonidae,† or barn owl family. One species, *Sophiornis quercynus*, was deemed distinctive enough to warrant the creation of a new family, the Sophiornithidae. This revision is significant since most authorities had considered the Miocene as supplying the first clear evidence of tytonid owls.

Here our sketch of the origin of owls must, alas, draw to a close. After the Quercy fauna fossil owls, along with all other prehistoric biota, begin to multiply exponentially, making even a telegraphic summary prohibitively long.

However, one more extinct owl, a fairly recent one, deserves special mention: *Ornimegalonyx*, a Cuban colossus—the biggest owl ever. Twice the size of a great horned owl, it was capable of killing giant ground sloths. Although Pleistocene Cuba had no major land predators, it did teem with huge herbivorous sloths and pig-sized rodents. *Ornimegalonyx* shared the job of keeping these brutes in check with an eagle larger than any known today, a vulture as big as an Andean condor, and two giant barn owls.

It was apparently only capable of weak flight, if it flew at all—a trait not unusual among insular birds. But with copious fare at talons' reach, powerful flight would have been needless luxury. An examination of only a portion of the fossil bones found in one small cave in the province of Las Villas yielded the remains of over two hundred individuals of the ground sloth *Mesocnus*. This cache and hundreds like it were almost certainly the result of *Ornimegalonyx* dragging its victims into underground dining rooms for an undisturbed repast.

One can imagine eagles and vultures loitering outside the cave, ready to horn in on *Ornimegalonyx*'s kill. At the entrance, *Cubacyon*, a jackal-like canid, scuttles about in the underbrush, whining. Raccoons squeal in the trees, while enormous barn owls perch, waiting for leftovers, deep inside the cave, whose travertine walls are besmirched with the droppings of hundreds of thousands of vampire bats. In the crevices slither the serpentine forms of Cuban boas.

Cave crawling in Cuba in the Pleistocene would have made even the Raiders of the Lost Ark take pause.

---

* Edentates ("toothless ones") are an order of mammals (Edentata) including sloths, armadillos, and the giant anteater of the Amazon.

† Mourer-Chauviré retains the traditional division of the owls in two separate families.

5

OWLS AROUND THE WORLD

Left: A northern hawk owl, a diurnal creature, perches atop a small spruce tree to scan the surrounding muskeg. Note the long tail feathers resembling those of hawks. Right: Two juvenile snowy owls hide amid arctic flowers after fledging their nearby nest in the Arctic National Wildlife Refuge in Alaska.

*A*ll but one of the nineteen North American owls either roam widely in other parts of the world or have close relatives in other lands that play similar roles in the drama of nocturnal predation.

A brief summary of how our owls fit in this mosaic will give a clear idea of the uniqueness or universality of each bird in a global perspective and will provide guidelines for a fuller appreciation of how the owls, collectively, parcel out the bounties of the biosphere.

The common barn owl comes close to being a true cosmopolite. It nests throughout the tropics and pushes well into the high latitudes of both temperate belts. Australasia is where the rest of the Tyto *owls reach their greatest diversity. Six of the eleven species in the group nest in this area. The handsome masked owl (*T. novahollandiae*), largest of the lot, is found in Australia, Tasmania, and a small part of New Guinea.*

Also classed in the barn owl subfamily are the two bizarre bay owls of the genus *Phodilus*. The African bay owl (*P. prigoginei*) is known from only one specimen collected in 1951 just west of Lake Tanganyika, in central Africa. The Oriental bay owl (*P. badius*), on the other hand, ranges all the way from India to Borneo.

Our most familiar owls, the eastern and western screech owls, as well as the whiskered owl and the flammulated owl, belong to the first group of the subfamily *Striginae*, in the genus *Otus*, which includes the scops owls of the Old World (twenty species) and the New World screech owls (eighteen species). Biologically very successful (almost every corner of the globe except the polar icecaps and the middle of the Sahara has a representative *Otus* owl), this group is a kaleidoscope of small tufted owls with exquisite plumage and distinctive voices. They also exhibit great genetic variability. Still rapidly evolving, they have radiated into a bewildering array of forms, many of which defy conventional classification. They are thus both a gold mine and a nightmare for the evolutionary biologist. One who has taken up the challenge with enthusiasm is Joe T. Marshall, Jr. Using bioacoustics as a key research tool, he has done much to unravel the taxonomic tangle of the screech owls. Largely as a result of Marshall's work, the western screech owl (*Otus kennicottii*) is now recognized as a separate species from the eastern screech owl (*O. asio*). A new screech owl, described from the Andes of Peru, has been named *Otus marshalli* in honor of their noted investigator. Another new screech owl, also from the Andes, has been baptized *Otus petersonii* even more recently, in honor of the peerless Roger Tory Peterson.

Ranked between the small screech owls and the giant eagle owls is the genus *Lophostrix*, consisting of two species—the West African maned owl (*L. lettii*) and the Central American crested owl (*L. cristata*), both beautiful medium-size "eared" owls that are especially intriguing, since they appear to be the remnants of a once flourishing phylogenetic bridge between screech and eagle owls.

Next in line are the eagle owls of the genus *Bubo*, formidable hunters commonly and justly dubbed "Tigers of the Air." Only one *Bubo* inhabits the New World, the great horned owl (*B. virginianus*), which nests from the Yukon River in north-central Alaska to the southern tip of South America. Throughout this vast range it is one of the best-known and most awe-inspiring birds of prey. The remaining *Bubos* thrive in different habitats throughout Europe, Africa, and Asia. The most impressive gives the group its name, the eagle owl (*B. bubo*), largest and most powerful of owls. Truly eagle-sized, it is capable of killing adult roe deer. This magnificent creature ranges from western Europe and North Africa to Siberia but is currently difficult to find except in remote and inaccessible localities, mostly in the higher mountains.

Closely related to *Bubo* is the equally big and powerful snowy owl (*Nyctea scandiaca*). Few birds have caught our fancy as vividly as this splendid white raptor. From ice-age cave dwellers to present-day Eskimos, this nemesis of the lemming and the arctic hare has held a prominent place in the imagination and the domestic economy of people inhabiting the boreal belt. Many of the finest productions of Eskimo art have been inspired by the snowy owl; the bird has also been a staple food since time immemorial.

Climbing up the phylogenetic tree we come to the pygmy owls of the genus *Glaucidium*, tiny birds that have been called sticks of dynamite with wings, and deservedly so.

The Eurasian pygmy owl (*G. passerinum*) and its North American counterpart, the northern pygmy owl (*G. gnoma*), are widespread and well-known species. Somewhat less so are the ferruginous and least pygmy owls (*G. brasilianum* and *G. minutissimum*). The first replaces the northern pygmy owl in arid habitat as far south as Guatemala and then nests south to Tierra del Fuego, with an odd gap in south-central South America. The second nests in separate areas of Mexico, Central America, and South America. Topping out at 5½ inches, it used to tie the elf owl (*Micrathene whitneyi*) of our southwestern deserts as the smallest owl in the world. Records, however, are made to be beaten. In 1976 the apparently inexhaustible treasure chest of the Andes yielded an improbably tiny mite of an owl, more diminutive even than the elf or the least pygmy. Bedecked with long filoplumes that radiate from the edges of the facial disks, it was christened the long-whiskered owlet, bearing the scientific name *Xenoglaux loweryi*.

Returning to the *Glaucidiums*, the Cuban pygmy owl (*G. siju*), an endemic species found only in Cuba and the Isle of Pines, is a fairly common and familiar bird. Three other *Glaucidium* owls from Africa and four from India and the Far East are less well known, although the pearl-spotted owlet (*G. perlatum*), widespread in the acacia woodlands of sub-Saharan Africa, is a common and conspicuous species.

Many of the medium-size owls of Australasia and Indonesia belong to a remarkable group of eighteen species known as the southern hawk owls. The genus *Ninox* contains the powerful owl (*N. strenua*) and the morepork owl or boobook (*N. novaseelandiae*), one of the most familiar birds down under. These are birds that have either retained or evolved distinctive hawklike traits (see Chapter 4, Evolution).

The only hawk owl (*Surnia ulula*) in the northern hemisphere is essentially an ecological counterpart of the similar Australasian birds, adapted to life in subarctic regions.

In the genus *Athene* we find one of the most famous of all birds. Albeit small, the little owl (*A. noctua*) was the mascot of the ancient Greeks and still nests in the vicinity of the Acropolis. Two other Old World congeners share its crepuscular hunting habits, undulating flight, and fossorial (burrowing) homemaking tendencies. All these traits can be found in the quaint New World burrowing owl (*A. cunicularia*).

The group of birds known as the wood owls consists of nineteen species in three genera. Of three colorful South American species in the genus *Pulsatrix*, the spectacled owl (*P. perspicillata*) is best known, probably because of its habit of haunting coffee plantations. Four owls in the genus *Ciccaba* are found in the New World tropics, the most familiar being the mottled owl (*C. virgata*), which ranges from Mexico to northern Argentina. The genus has one representative in Africa, the African wood owl (*C. woodfordii*), widespread south of the Sahara. Five of the eleven owls in the genus *Strix* inhabit the northern temperate belt, three live in the tropical areas of Asia, two are South American, and one is restricted to desert wadis in the Near and Middle East. This genus boasts some of the top stars in the strixine firmament, namely, the tawny owl (*S. aluco*), the "to-whit, to-whoo" bird of Shakespearean fame; the great gray owl (*S. nebulosa*), majestic "phantom of the northern forest," as Robert Nero fittingly dubbed it; and the barred owl (*S. varia*), vocalist nonpareil and the "whangdoodle" of Dixie folklore.

The genus *Asio* comprises six species in two ecologically distinct categories: long-eared owls—mostly dark-hued nocturnal birds that breed in forests; and short-eared owls—typically pale diurnal birds that nest and hunt in open country. The prototype of the first group is the long-eared owl (*A. otus*), distributed all along the northern hemisphere between latitudes 30° and 65° north. The short-eared owl (*A. flammeus*), champion flyer among owls, represents the second group throughout an enormous range that encompasses the northern hemisphere between latitudes 40° and 70° north and the southern half of South America, with isolated populations in the West Indies, Hawaii, the Galapagos, and the delta of the Orinoco.

The island of Jamaica has the distinction of harboring a genus of its own, *Pseudoscops,* with one species, the Jamaican owl (*P. grammicus*). A medium-size forest dweller, it is sometimes linked to the preceding *Asio* owls and sometimes to the following genus.

The final group in this sketch of the world's owls and their distribution contains the four very small owls of the genus *Aegolius,* featuring two quite well-known birds and two about which a good deal remains to be discovered. These last two, not surprisingly, are found in the New World tropics—the unspotted saw-whet owl (*A. ridgwayi*) in mountains from southern Mexico to Costa Rica, and the buff-fronted owl (*A. harrisii*) in two apparently separate areas of northwestern and east central South America. Much better known are the boreal owl (*A. funereus*), of circumpolar distribution (known as Tengmalm's owl in Europe), and the lovely saw-whet owl (*A. hudsonicus*), from the humid forests of North America.

An adult great horned owl at nest with three owlets.

6

THE OWLS OF NORTH AMERICA

A Portfolio

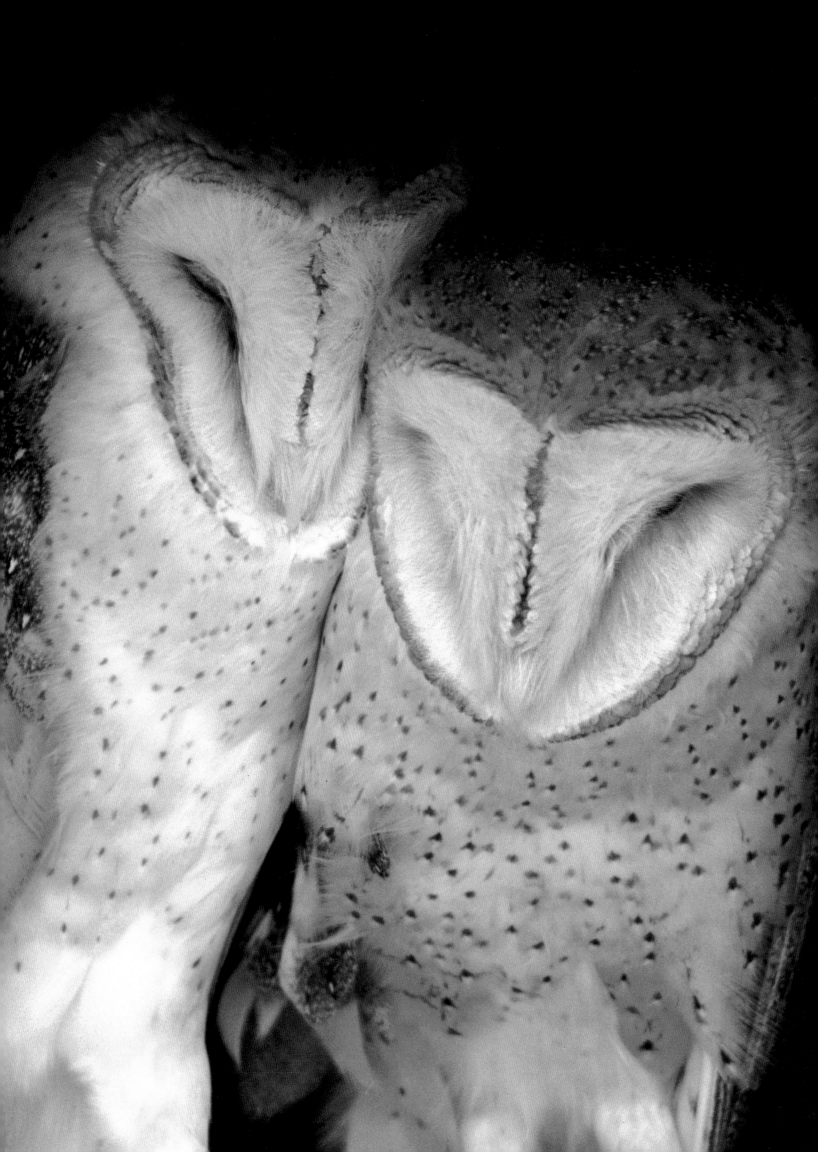

COMMON BARN OWL
(*Tyto alba*)

Left: Barn owls roosting in the dark recesses of an old barn in Washington State. Right: Typical barn owl habitat—an old barn surrounded by grain fields.

DESCRIPTION Size 14–21 inches; wingspan 41–47 inches. A slender, long-legged, medium-size "earless" owl with a distinctive white heart-shaped facial disk rimmed with tan. Eyes are dark and almond shaped. Golden buff above; back shows pearl-gray patches stippled with white-rimmed "eyelets." Mostly white below, lightly speckled with dark spots; breast can show buff wash. Looks ghostly seen at night from below. Dark race buff below and on face, darker back.

VOICE Remarkably varied. Most often heard are shrill snoring hisses—*kksssch!*—at nest or roost (uttered both by adults and young; often compared to escaping steam); an abrasive shriek—*ssshnaairrkk!*—sometimes given in flight; another flight call, a snarling *cliaaakk!*—metallic clicks and rattles. Migrants utter a sharply enunciated *whesshhpp!*—a blend of the hiss and hunting scream.

SIMILAR SPECIES Snowy owl larger, rotund, dome-headed; pure white or barred with black or tan; yellow-eyed. Short-eared owl dark-faced, heavily streaked; in flight shows dark carpal patches ("wrists"), more bull-necked profile; also yellow-eyed.

RANGE Almost cosmopolitan. In New World nests from southern British Columbia east across North Dakota, southern Michigan, extreme southern Ontario, southwestern Quebec, and central New England south throughout the United States to Mexico and the West Indies; through Central and South America south to Tierra del Fuego.

HABITAT Widespread in open country, such as prairies, savannahs, marshes, farmland, and deserts; also forages in suburban parklands and residential areas. Roosts and nests in caves, mine shafts, culverts, cliffs, holes in trees, silos, barns, and derelict buildings and unused structures. Accepts nesting boxes.

NESTING Almost year-round; most egg laying between March and June. Incubation 32–34 days; fledging 40–50 days. Double-brooded in warmer parts of range, when prey is abundant.

Many individuals in northern part of range (both adults and juveniles) disperse southward in winter. East-west and west-east wandering in late autumn also noted.

PREY Chiefly rodents and shrews, but also takes reptiles, birds (very few), and bats.

Top: A barn owl nest containing three eggs and a single one-day-old hatchling; prey (a mouse) is adjacent to the nest. Above: A female barn owl incubating in its nest (egg is visible at bottom). Above right: A barn owl with seven owlets. Right: A parent bird delivers prey to two owlets. This species has been nicknamed "The Flying Mousetrap."

NATURAL HISTORY

The barn owl is an unmistakable and exquisite bird, and, as one of the best mousers, unquestionably a beneficial one. Farmers throughout the world have learned to appreciate it as such. Programs to protect the birds and promote their nesting have been launched in many rural areas. "Barnies," however, perform their useful services in ways that do not always endear them to man.

Hunting barn owls are often seen quartering silently over meadows and fields in low-altitude flights. Not infrequently, however, they will startle the observer (and presumably their prey) with one of the rasping, drawn-out screams described above. More than one vexed

farmer, deciding to get rid of rodents in a less disconcerting way, has shot his resident barn owl and replaced it with a tabby. What happens next is that the owl gets stuffed and stuck on the mantelpiece, the tabby has litter after litter of kittens, and the farmer remains blissfully ignorant of the fact that *one* pair of nesting barn owls can eliminate more mice per night than *ten* cats put together!

It is possible that hunting barn owls scream to flush out animals lurking in dense and probably damp grass. Wet ground is known to impair the hunting efficiency of these owls, whose hearing plays a major role in securing prey. Rain-soaked leaves, grass, or earth muffle the telltale patter of voles and shrews skittering along grassy runways or thrashing about in leaf litter. At nesting time the hunting powers of parent birds are taxed to the utmost. With a batch of hungry babies and a couple of days of steady rain, the barn owl must resort to novel tactics to overcome a handicap. Startling a lethargic vole by uttering an unexpected shriek may be one such trick.

Barn owls are inventive opportunists par excellence. Their flexibility will be explored in greater detail in the section on behavior (Chapter 8). Here it is enough to point out that they have been known to thrive on such diverse fare as rats, rails, storm petrels, and terns; that they have been observed to catch these creatures with equal adeptness by day and by night; and that the sites of their successful hunting forays have been as eclectic as atolls, caves, rice fields, and airport runways.

The clicking call referred to previously has been noted by Lewis Wayne Walker and others as being uttered by mated pairs prior to copulation. Other observers, myself included, have heard "barnies" making this sound while flying in circles around, or fairly close to, known roosts or nesting sites. An odd fact is that instances have been recorded of the birds seeming actually to *aim* the sound in the air, sometimes at specific structures, sometimes at nothing in particular. This peculiar behavior has suggested to no less an authority on barn owls than Roger Payne that the birds may in fact be capable of some form of echolocation. This is the "sonar" mechanism, so highly evolved in bats and dolphins, that enables the animal to avoid obstacles and find prey in situations of poor visibility. The notion, of course, must be tested experimentally.

FLAMMULATED OWL
(*Otus flammeolus*)

Left: The mottled feathers of an adult flammulated owl are perhaps one of the best examples of camouflage. The small owl blends perfectly with the rough texture of the trunk. Right: An adult flammulated owl delivers food to fledglings. These tiny owls just over five inches in length thrive predominantly on insects.

DESCRIPTION

Size 6–7 inches; wingspan 14–19 inches. Smallest "eared" owl in North America; eyes dark brown; ear tufts inconspicuous. Crown, nape, and upper back like weathered bark: a variegated, mottled gray or gray-brown with dusky streaking. White scapular spots with broad rufous edging form paired shoulder stripes that meet above rump, creating a distinctive V. Wings and tail narrowly banded. Breast and belly pale ashy, heavily furrowed with dark streaks and crossbars. Birds range from gray in north of range to reddish in south; gray owls may show little rusty coloring; "bright" birds have facial disks with broad rufous borders and many feathers with russet edgings. Toes are unfeathered.

VOICE

A remarkably low-pitched, mellow, single or double hoot—*shoop* or *who-WHOOP* (also transcribed as *boo-BOOT*)—with leisurely delivery (2–8 second pauses), interspersed with three-syllable variants—*boot-oop, POOP* or *bottle-oop, POOP*. Quality seldom harsh, but some birds sing with muted gruffness approaching soft bark. Other calls include kitten-like mewing, clucking sounds during courtship, and, rarely, a screech.

SIMILAR SPECIES

Whiskered owl and western screech owl larger, yellow-eyed; lack rusty facial disks and reddish shoulder stripes; both have feathered toes and very different voices (best "fieldmark").

RANGE

Breeds from southern British Columbia south along mountains to Arizona, New Mexico, and western Texas; through western Mexico south to Guatemala. Nests locally in southern California. Northern populations presumed to winter mostly south of the border.

HABITAT

Western mountain forests, showing strong preference for ponderosa pines with nearby thickets; also in pine-oak habitats—white oaks favorite roosting trees.

NESTING

Usually in abandoned woodpecker hole or other tree cavity. Eggs 2–4, early May to late June. Smaller clutches predominate.

MIGRATION   Generally considered to be strongly migratory, with most of the individuals from extensive northern range presumably flying south in winter to Mexico and Central America. Vagrant to Louisiana, Alabama, and Florida.

PREY   Almost exclusively insects, many, including sphinx moths, caught on the wing; also spiders, caterpillars, scorpions; very little evidence of predation on mammals or birds.

NATURAL HISTORY

In a tribe famed for cunningly disguised ferocity the flammulated owl takes top prize for gentleness. It is a shy, retiring bird, seldom indulging in the demonstrative antics of its congeners, the whiskered and western screech owls, and decidedly incapable of matching the rapacity of the pygmy owls.

It feeds almost entirely on insects. This choice of food is shared by many other raptors, but no other owl in North America is so predominantly insectivorous.

The flammulated owl has mastered the art of hunting on the wing. From a perch deep in a pine or oak it will wait for a sphinx moth to hover nearby. The alert eyes of the owl will follow each move of the moth unerringly.

Suddenly, at the exact moment that offers maximum precision, the owl zooms out and snatches the moth in midair. The performance, like a flycatcher's, shows speed and agility remarkable for an owl.

Essentially, this is what flammulated owls do for a living. It is a life-style that requires special adaptations. One is obvious. No insect-eating bird can conceivably survive the rigors of winter in this owl's montane habitat. It is thus forced either to seek food in warmer climates or to adopt some other strategy for survival. Other owls stage migratory flights, but none approach the range and regularity of the flammulated owls' annual movements. The idea, however, has been proposed by N. K.

Left: A flammulated owl incubates eggs in its nest cavity—like those of many small owls, taken over from woodpeckers. Below: A flammulated owl, bearing food, returns to the nest.

Johnson that this species may not be a long-distance migrant after all and that its apparent absence from breeding areas in winter may be due to torpidity (various degrees and durations of lowered metabolic rate) or actual long-term hibernation. The latter has been proved in the poorwill (*Phalaenoptilus nuttallii*), a nightjar closely related to the owls. Hibernation in an owl is an intriguing idea, but one that needs further study.

The other important adaptation to insect catching, less obvious but perhaps more interesting, is structural modification. In this species evolution has sacrificed the sturdy skeleton and heavy-duty talons of other owls in favor of speed, buoyancy, and mobility. The flammulated owl's bones are extremely light and brittle. Even the skull is comparatively thin. The very small, tapered body and tiny, stubby "ears" minimize wind drag. Muscle and tendon mechanisms are built for swift action, not massive power.

Vis-à-vis larger owls and other predators, this is a creature that clearly cannot hold its own in a fight. It is often a meal for the spot-ted owl. Long-eared owls also willingly add it to their menu. And any hawk that happens to see one will have no trouble crunching its friable body as if it were a pretzel. Mercifully—for both the owl and the birders who delight in its subtle beauty—Mother Nature has provided for its survival. Most owls are superbly camouflaged, the flammulated almost perfectly so. Edouard Jacot, a diligent early student of Arizona's owls, wrote: "It is greatly assisted in avoiding detection by the color of its plumage. The owl's back blends perfectly with the bark of the pine tree, and the markings of its underparts with that of the white oak at night, so that it is almost invisible when it is perched with its back toward the stem of the tree."

Thus the flammulated owl thrives in verdant mountain forests, serving as nature's check on the prolific moths and affording lovers of natural beauty a glimpse of the delicate design described by A. C. Bent as their "prettily variegated color pattern of browns, silvery gray, black, white, and cinnamon."

Left: A flammulated owl arrives at the nest, where an owlet begs for food. Top: Flammulated owl hatchlings. Above: Flammulated owlet with its meal in its beak.

EASTERN SCREECH OWL
(*Otus asio*)

Left: A red-phase eastern screech owl spotted in New York State momentarily perches at the entrance to its nest cavity. Right: A red-phase eastern screech owl roosts on an old stump in an eastern deciduous forest.

DESCRIPTION
Size 7–10 inches; wingspan 18–24 inches. Only small eastern owl with ear tufts; some owls seldom raise them. Dichromatic: both red and gray owls have facial disks edged in black, yellow eyes, light-hued bills, two rows of white wing spots, lightly barred primaries, and faintly banded tails. Red owls are fox red or rich rust above; whitish below with rufous crossbars and dark vertical streaks; rufous facial disks. Gray birds are steel to ash gray or gray-brown above, often with patches of light brown; darker on crown; heavily streaked and crossbarred; underparts whitish; gray patches with dark vertical shafts and crossbars are prominent on upper breast, sometimes creating open vest effect; lower belly much less streaked. A very pale gray race (*O. a. maxwelliae*) occurs in northwestern extremity of range. Intermediate plumages not uncommon. Most juveniles have wavy horizontal bars without streaks.

VOICE
A descending whinny, like a miniature toy horse, associated with aggression and territorial defense; a single rolling trill on one pitch, sometimes accelerating and growing louder toward end, associated with courtship and nest defense. Males and females sing trill duets in mating season; males lower pitched. Snappy, barklike whistle serves as alarm-contact call for fledglings. Extraordinary variety of calls during distraction displays by parents defending young.

SIMILAR SPECIES
In small zone of overlap (central Texas) with western screech owl, gray birds of both species told apart only by voice.

RANGE
Nests from southeastern Saskatchewan east along Canadian border to New England, south along east coast to Florida; along eastern foothills of Rocky Mountains to central Texas and eastern Mexico.

HABITAT
Open woodlands, forest clearings, old orchards, suburban parklands. Fond of old trees with knotholes. Not shy.

NESTING In old woodpecker holes, natural cavities, or birdhouses (flicker boxes with sawdust bottom ideal). Eggs 3–8 (average, 4–5) from February to July in vast range; in central U.S. between April and June. Incubation by female alone 26–28 days; young fly 4 weeks after hatching.

MIGRATION Mostly resident. Some withdrawal in winter from northern parts of range. Some wandering (postbreeding dispersal) in autumn.

PREY Virtually omnivorous, except for plants. Will take small mammals, birds, small fish, reptiles, amphibians, and a vast array of insects, centipedes, and other arthropods.

Eastern screech owl.

NATURAL HISTORY

Until recently the eastern screech owl and its western counterpart were considered to be a single polymorphic species—one that had evolved into many distinct races. Current consensus classifies birds west of the Rocky Mountains as a separate species (*Otus kennicottii*) with many local variants. Joe Marshall, screech owl expert nonpareil, has proposed an ingenious breakdown into species, subspecies, and "emergent species." In this book a simplified treatment will be used, emphasizing what the two main groups of owls have in common. Consequently, anything said about the lifestyle of eastern screech owls will apply to western birds, unless otherwise noted.

Screech owls do not ordinarily screech. They produce, on the contrary, some very attractive sounds. The double trill of western birds and the long single trill of their eastern cousins are often heard in duet form. Males and females many times begin and end in perfect synchrony. In eastern birds the trills are sometimes pitched at harmonic intervals of a third or a fifth, a soothing woodland song if ever there was one. On moonlit April nights, when tree frogs and toads break the news of fresh life stirring on the still cold ground, the duets of screech owls in the branches of a willow or a cottonwood, overarching marsh or stream, are a true aerial obbligato to the lusty chorus of amphibians throbbing below.

Screech owls do, albeit very rarely, screech, or more precisely, go vocally berserk. These outbursts are restricted to the brief period when their babies, still mostly tailless and very vulnerable, have just left the nest and are beginning to learn to fly. The parents keep close watch over their fluffy darlings. And woe betide the birder who gets too close! Many an intrepid owl watcher has left part of his or her scalp in the claws of an infuriated mama owl. In all fairness to the scalpers, screech owls almost never do physical damage without giving the intruder plenty of warning—this by way of an astounding mixture of squawks, squeals, grunts, and wails that, rather than the vocalizations of a pair of typically rather quiet little birds, sound like the outpourings of a pack of demented raccoons. (It must be added that many kinds of owls, including the otherwise dignified great gray owl, indulge in distraction displays much like this.)

Screech owls are exceptional hunters. They consistently catch prey as diverse as crayfish and salamanders; rats, mice, and shrews; all manner of beetles, crickets, and moths; small fish (they wade readily in shallow water) and birds. The latter range from regularly and steadily obtained snacks of songbirds like vireos, warblers, and sparrows to occasional gluttonous feasts on blue grouse in the west and ruffed grouse in the east. There is even a documented case of screech owls dining for days on domestic bantam chickens! Concerning the taking of songbirds, it is important to make clear that screech owls catch them only when they have young to feed (pygmy owls do the same) and that even when predation is heavy the total population of songbirds in the area is not impaired. With regard to domestic fowl, it must be remembered that all predators are opportunists: if a poorly tended chicken coop allows an owl access to a tempting morsel, the henkeeper is to blame.

The Niche Switch

A fascinating feature in the natural history of these and many other owls is one colloquially dubbed the "niche switch."

The predilection screech owls show for woodland borders facing open fields, and their use of tree holes for roosting and nesting, make them in many cases the nocturnal equivalent of the American kestrel, smallest and most brightly colored of our falcons. Also a tree-hole nester, the kestrel often agrees with the screech owl in choice of food. Both, for example, are fond of crickets.

This correspondence between a hunter that finds its prey by daylight and another that takes over the same hunting ground at night is the niche switch. We shall come across it again and again as we explore the life of owls. It is an excellent example of what ecology is all about.

Plants and animals cluster in patterns, known as ecosystems, determined by such things as soil profile, terrain, and climate. Ecosystems typically produce an excess of each of their characteristic components. But properly functioning ecosystems do not allow waste: an overabundance of crickets, for instance, may feed the kestrel by day, but many are left over to be taken at night. This creates what is called an ecological niche, an "opening" in the economy of the system, much like a job opening requiring special talents. And just so the job will not go begging, nature, the greatest talent scout and employment agent of all, has come up with a "nocturnal kestrel"—the screech owl.

That the winsome screech owl should be partner in predation to the pretty little kestrel is most appropriate, for in looks and personality the owl is at least a match for the falcon.

Take feathering, for example. The kestrel, with its black heraldic cheek marks, bright russet back and tail, slate-blue crown and steel-blue wings, is famed for beauty of plumage. Next to it a healthy red screech owl can surely hold its own. But the subtler gray birds are also extraordinary. Indeed, for splendid cryptic plumage the screech owls, regardless of color, rival the nightjars. In both groups, shafts, spots, daggers, bars, and meshes in black, burgundy, and brown seem to have been penciled in with precision on a lighter-hued background where soft tones of buff, tawny brown, and creamy white predominate.

The poorwill, a nightjar common in the West, roosts on rocky ground. Its plumage matches stones and pebbles so beautifully that Joe Marshall has called it "the best example of cryptic coloration in the animal kingdom." Just so does the screech owl mimic tree bark to perfection. As the poorwill is the king of camouflage on the ground, the screech owl is the monarch of disguise in the trees above.

Eastern screech owl.

WESTERN SCREECH OWL
(*Otus kennicottii*)

Left: Two western screech owls perch on branch stubs of an old-growth cedar tree. Right: Typical screech owl habitat—open woodland terrain.

DESCRIPTION   Virtually identical to eastern screech owl but a bit larger (may reach 11 inches in length), with more prominent dark streaking above and below. Gray to gray-brown; red form (very rare) found only in Puget Sound race. Pacific Northwest owls large and dark; desert birds smaller and paler. Bills usually dark except in Canadian birds.

VOICE   A series of short, hollow whistles with wooden quality, starting up slowly then speeding up, with notes running together, ending in a brief, fine roll. Final roll strong in coastal subspecies; fainter, sometimes lacking in inland races. Often dubbed the "bouncing ball" call (in reference to initial, leisurely "bops" of rubber ball dropped from height), which increases in speed and fades out in a quick roll. Mating call a double trill, the first part short, the second longer; often given in duet form. As with eastern owls, a large repertoire of yelps, barklike whistles, wails.

SIMILAR SPECIES   See eastern screech owl. In southwestern canyon lands, told from whiskered owl by voice; from dark-eyed flammulated owl by yellow eyes, larger size, feathered toes.

RANGE   From extreme southern Alaska south along Pacific Slope to Baja California and Sinaloa; east in the interior to central British Columbia; south through most of West (including western Rockies), down to central Texas (Big Bend) and south to central Mexico.

HABITAT   Much like eastern screech owl. Desert races use holes in yuccas and cacti or willows and cottonwoods along streams; also in pinyon oak–juniper habitats.

NESTING   Like eastern screech owl.

MIGRATION   None; some postbreeding dispersal.

PREY   Like eastern screech owl. Desert species such as scorpions and lizards are important in diet of southwestern birds.

Above: Screech owl fledglings perch on a tree branch just outside their nest cavity, displaying branching behavior, while a single fledgling remains inside the cavity.
Right: Screech owlets perch on a tree branch (more branching behavior). Far right: A pair of screech owlets begins to display branching activity.

NATURAL HISTORY

The habits of western screech owls closely match those of their eastern counterparts. Like the latter, they are versatile raptors. Almost any small mammal, bird, or insect can be fair game for this little flying wildcat. Western "screechies" have even been known to catch and kill creatures as large as blue grouse.

This species features a complex array of races, each corresponding to a specific region. The largest and darkest birds are found in moist, cool Northwest forests, the palest and smallest in desert washes in the Southwest and Mexico. This is a good illustration of Bergmann's Rule—in a polymorphic warm-blooded species, body size increases as ambient temperature decreases (cools). In larger birds, body surface is smaller in proportion to volume, so that heat is conserved during cold spells. Smaller birds have greater body surface in proportion to volume, helping them to cool off through heat loss.

It is in the canyons of southeastern Arizona and southwestern New Mexico (a region that bids fair to be the best owl study area in the U.S.) that the *Otus* owls reach their apogee. Here the screech owls prefer willows and cottonwoods at low to mid-altitudes; whiskered owls favor higher country (4,000–6,000 feet); while flammulated owls are quite content in elevations of up to 9,000 feet.

A fledgling western screech owlet flies from branch to branch in the process of strengthening its wings.

WHISKERED OWL
(*Otus trichopsis*)

Left: A whiskered owl roosts in a branch near the bole of a tree, which provides camouflage. Right: An alert whiskered owl perches on a tree branch while searching for food.

DESCRIPTION	Size 6.5–8 inches; wingspan 16–20 inches. A bit smaller but strikingly similar to gray Southwest race of screech owl. Facial bristles longer; bigger white spots on wings, coarser mottling, heavier streaks on underparts; ear tufts and feet smaller. These marks noticeable only in hand-held specimens or at point-blank range under ideal viewing conditions. Best fieldmark is voice.
VOICE	Territorial call—series of 4–6 short, mellow, "hooty" whistles on one pitch, delivered at even rhythm about as fast as one can count them, not unlike sound produced by blowing across open bottle; often transcribed as *boot-boot-boot-boot*. Similar call of screech owl speeds up; whiskered stays even, may slow down at end. Mating song, often delivered in duet form, strikingly like Morse code—a series of irregularly accented single and double notes, often in short groups of three, a pause, then a fourth, longer terminal note; many other patterns. Alarm notes many and varied.
SIMILAR SPECIES	Screech owl, separable by voice, usually in open woods at lower altitudes; whiskered mostly in dense oak groves above 4,000 feet. Tiny flammulated owl dark-eyed, usually above 6,000 feet; different voice.
RANGE	In mountains of southeastern Arizona and southwest New Mexico south to Central America.
HABITAT	Dense oak groves, sycamores, and oak-pine associations in high canyon country, often close to stream-side thickets.
NESTING	Natural cavity or abandoned flicker hole in oaks and sycamores. Eggs 3–4, late April to early May. Incubation and hatching probably by female. Fledglings probably by early to mid-June.
MIGRATION	Mostly resident.

PREY Moths (a staple item at nesting time) and beetles taken in flight; caterpillars, grasshoppers, crickets, beetle larvae, spiders, and scorpions caught on leaves, branches, and ground. Centipedes, mole crickets, and scorpions are key winter foods. Takes few small mammals.

NATURAL HISTORY

Whiskered owls instantly recall the romance of roaming at night through canyons in the Huachucas and Chiricahuas, those marvelous Arizona mountains, where their Morse code tootings echo across the clean, crisp air. This owl, indeed, is one of the most sought-after species in such bird-finding meccas as Cave Creek Canyon, in the outskirts of Tucson, along with such other southeastern Arizona specialties as the elegant trogon and the elf owl.

In canyon country the whiskered owl may now and then overlap the domain of the western screech owl. When this happens the two

Left: A whiskered owl holds prey in the form of a caterpillar in its beak. The whiskered owl's diet consists mainly of insects. Above: A female whiskered owl peers out from its nesting cavity thirty feet above the ground in a sycamore tree. Nests are found in deep tree cavities or flicker holes and contain 3 to 4 eggs.

species tend to segregate ecologically. Screech owls prefer the edges of open woods and show a strong bias for vertebrate prey such as rodents, reptiles, and birds. Whiskered owls, on the other hand, feel most at home in the thickest inner sections of an oak grove and are happiest when roosting in the shelter of the densest foliage. They also show a marked preference for crunchy food, to wit, arthropods, and eat moths with much greater relish than mice.

In this manner, the whiskered and screech owls divvy up the morsels in nature's smorgasbord; they can stuff themselves and feed their babies without coming to blows over a mutually coveted delicacy. This parceling out of living space and prey illustrates how the adoption of separate ecological niches permits sibling species to exploit an apparently identical resource without threatening each other's survival.

One behavior seems unusual enough to deserve comment. Whereas screech and flammulated owls respond to territorial challenges mostly in the trees they live in, whiskered owls have several times been observed to do battle—or in any case *offer* to do battle—on the ground. This has been the experience of birders who have induced territorial defense by playing tape recordings of whiskered owl songs while standing in moderately large clearings. Perhaps the explanation lies in the owl's exceedingly keen hearing, which leads it directly to the source of the sound—the tape recorder, often held at waist height. Whiskered owls will also sometimes waddle up to a man whistling an imitation of their song; Joe Marshall tells of feisty males strutting close enough to be picked up. And they have been known to land on a picnic table and march resolutely toward a cassette player, clearly believing that a rival was hiding inside!

GREAT HORNED OWL
(*Bubo virginianus*)

Left: An adult great horned owl. Right: Typical great horned owl habitat—dense wooded areas of conifers or hardwoods.

DESCRIPTION Size 18–25 inches; wingspan 35–55 inches. Females larger. Heaviest and most powerful American owl. A very large, bulky bird with prominent, widely spaced ear tufts; large, bright yellow eyes framed by typically tawny facial disks (pale in Arctic race); and bold white throat bib. Color ranges from very dark (Pacific Northwest, Canadian Maritimes) to sandy (desert races) or almost white (Arctic). Typical birds mottled above with rich pattern of chestnut, black, and grayish white; buff below, with heavy, dark brown horizontal barring.

VOICE Typically 3–6 deep, resonant hoots in many arrangements. A common format: male sings full-voiced hoot, follows with cluster of quickly uttered pulsing hoots, ends with two longer, full-voiced hoots—*HOO! hu-hu-hu HOO-HOO!*; female answers with slightly higher, shorter sequence. (Lower pitch, greater complexity of male's call only recently ascertained.) Courting couples select special perch to sing duets at dawn and dusk. Pause between male's call and female's reply gets shorter as pair formation nears climax; songs of mated pairs often overlap. Nestlings have loud, throaty bark. First summer siblings call for food and stay in touch with sharp, husky whistle—*scheeeakk!*—or raspy blend of whistle and scream—*khreek!*—tirelessly repeated from late afternoon well into the night, often with many variations, including catlike meows. Aggression displays accompanied by bill snapping, loud hissing, large repertoire of growls, grunts, and squeals. Capable of blood-curdling scream, seldom given.

SIMILAR SPECIES Long-eared owl smaller and slimmer, ear tufts set closer together, has vertical streaks (not horizontal bars) below, lacks white throat. Other medium-to-large owls are "earless." Arctic race sometimes confused with snowy owl. Horned owls usually in trees; snowy owls usually in open country.

RANGE Throughout North and South America, from tundra tree line south to Tierra del Fuego.

HABITAT   Remarkably adaptable. Wide variety of environments, from deep forests, desert cliffs, and woodlots to suburban estates, parks, and cemeteries. Roosts in dense foliage, tree holes, old nests, cliff ledges, et cetera, from sea level to 11,000 feet.

NESTING   In old nests of hawks, herons, eagles, or crows; ledges in cliffs and rocky crevices; large cavities in trees. Often uses abandoned nests of red-tailed hawks; regularly usurps active nests of this species; owlets have been reared in corner of active bald eagle's nest. Eggs 1–6, usually 2–3, laid as early as January and February in New England. Incubation by both sexes, 25–30 days. Young fly 9–10 weeks after hatching, often spend 10 days to 2 weeks on ground (where fed and defended by parents) before full flight capability.

MIGRATION   Essentially sedentary. Some withdrawal from extreme northern limit of range in severe winters. Outside breeding season some individuals may wander widely.

PREY   Amazingly varied but has distinct preference for rabbits, rats, and mice, depending on locality and cyclic abundance. List includes opossums, muskrats, woodchucks, squirrels, gophers, and meadow mice; known to kill porcupines, cats, and skunks. Also large birds like ducks, geese, swans, herons, pheasant, grouse, turkeys, and chickens; medium-size birds such as woodpeckers, orioles, and jays; and many kinds of hawks and owls (on which it is a severe limiting factor). Eats snakes, frogs, crayfish, and many kinds of fish; takes large insects like beetles and locusts and such other arthropods as scorpions. Predation on songbirds minimal, but kills large numbers of crows by strafing their roosts at night and will even descend chimneys to catch swifts.

NATURAL HISTORY

The strixine Nimrod, powerful, fearless, resourceful, the great horned owl outwits and outmaneuvers virtually all other hunting birds that may choose to match talons and talents with it. In its domain, only the golden eagle can compete for the title of top avian raptor.

In fact, great horned owls are probably the most successful predators in North America. They will not hesitate to take on a bobcat, fight a fox, or even tussle with a coyote. Even if the owl loses, the large mammal will know it has been in a real fight.

The great horned owl's success has not been achieved without detriment to other birds of prey. Cliffs where peregrine falcons used to nest in pre-DDT days have been rendered useless for their reintroduction now that the threat of pesticide pollution has been reduced. Why? Horned owls have colonized the cliffs so thickly that the release of young peregrines is futile. Reducing their number by capture is just about impossible. Even in situations where they coexist with other birds of prey, horned owls hog both space and food supply.

This will be viewed with either wonder or a jaundiced eye, depending on the viewer. To the reintroduction specialist, armed with federal funds and foundation grants to create new nesting sites for bald eagles, peregrines, or osprey, a failed mission can mean loss of live-

lihood. It's a safe bet then that the great horned owl will be stigmatized as a wanton, vicious killer, and strategies for checking its depredations will be vigorously urged. On the other hand, someone with a strong bias against management might see the owl's triumphant spread as vindication of the notion of noninterference with nature's checks and balances.

What we have here, undeniably, is a case of survival of the fittest—and great horned owls are fit indeed. In the last half century they have shown a startling ability to adapt to the drastic changes wrought by our invasion of their primeval haunts. Landfills and dumps on the outskirts of cities are ideal for the proliferation of rats and scavengers like gulls and crows; the great horned owl feasts on all three. Artificial impoundments—be they reservoirs, industrial park or shopping mall ponds, or lakes in suburban parks and estates—are magnets for waterfowl, wading birds, and gulls (not to mention muskrats), all of which are gourmet fare for this bird. Suburban development, indeed, creates a supermarket full of opossums, raccoons, skunks, squirrels, chipmunks, shrews, mice, and rats—all of which the horned owl will readily toss into its shopping cart.

Nesting sites are hardly scarce. Any reduction of hawk nests through human disturbance is compensated by a great increase of crow and squirrel nests.

Above left: A great horned owl perches in a crabapple tree. During daylight hours, great horned owls often roost in dense trees to escape harassment by crows and jays. Above right: Two juvenile great horned owlets await the return of a parent. Right: A great horned owl fledgling on the ground amid balsamroot. When young owls fledge from the nest, they often land on the ground below. Soon they begin hopping up the branches of adjacent trees.

The dark side of the picture is garden pesticides. An increased use of toxic broad-spectrum chemicals has again in recent years conjured up the specter of insidious environmental poisoning.

The great horned owl is a clear indicator of this problem. Poisoned owls are turning up at an alarming rate. Just before writing these lines the author picked up a young male in the throes of a seizure probably caused by organochlorine pesticide poisoning. Fortunately the bird revived, but many are not so lucky.

An intriguing aspect of *Bubo*'s success story is its apparent owlish wisdom. In twenty years of studying this species, virtually every nest I have seen has been in or close to estates belonging to members of the National Audubon Society, in wildlife refuges, or in protected public lands. Why? Simple, you might say: these are areas frequented by bird-lovers, and dramatic species like great horned owls will therefore be looked for—and found. But at least 75 percent of these nests were found, completely by chance, by nonbirders!

Clearly, some sort of adaptive mechanism is at work here. What stimuli—or absence of stimuli—do the owls manage to sense that tells them the area is a safe one in which to bring up young? Is it year-round absence of firearm activity? Absence (or low numbers) of roaming dogs (a threat to owlets on the ground)? Low levels of noise and traffic? Whatever the case, something in sanctuary-type environments registers with the owls' "antennae," leading them to set up housekeeping there in preference to sites where they would be far more vulnerable. Call it wisdom, call it "site selection based on subliminal detection of low incidence of life-threatening elements" (behavioral biologists do talk funny), the fact is that this king of American owls is a hugely successful animal, compared to less flexible species such as the whooping crane and the ivory-billed woodpecker. A fair share of this success must be attributed to the horned owl's mysterious but nonetheless undeniable capacity for homesteading where the likelihood of disturbance is minimal, if not absent altogether.

The Niche Switch

In many rural areas the great horned owl is the nocturnal equivalent of the red-tailed hawk. Both show a preference for higher ground than the barred owl and the red-shouldered hawk, raptors that share the bounties provided by bottomland woods. These last two species often nest simultaneously in the same tract. Horned owls, in contrast, don't

get along with red-tailed hawks. In fact, they so often harry and even kill these hapless hawks that a red-tail, given half a chance, will not hesitate to try to exterminate a great horned owl.

But it isn't just the large and powerful red-tails that come in for a share of horned owl harassment. With the exception of the golden

eagle, *all* birds of prey are in awe of its ferocity, formidable talons, and murderous beak.

This fact has created a most unusual—and remarkably effective—tool for the student of raptor bird populations. Just about every hawk in the land responds dramatically to a calling horned owl. If the hooting is loud enough, it will draw out virtually any territorial hawk lurking in a wooded tract of quite considerable size. Students canvassing hawk populations at nesting time chug along backroads in four-wheel-drive vehicles with roof-mounted loudspeakers or take to the woods toting "boom boxes"—all with the goal of flushing out hawks by magnifying the already far-carrying love calls of the "tiger of the air."

SNOWY OWL
(Nyctea scandiaca)

*Left: A snowy owl.
Right: The snowy owl lives in the open tundra of the arctic, where it nests upon small mounds or hillocks that protect the nest somewhat from the damp ground.*

DESCRIPTION   Size 20–24 inches; wingspan 54–66 inches. A very large white owl with golden yellow eyes, no ear tufts. Adult males almost pure white; larger females more or less heavily barred with blackish brown. Juveniles (often seen in southward flights) darker than adults; first-year females especially dark, except for pure white face, nape, and upper breast, which stand out in sharp contrast with densely barred body and heavily spotted crown. Exceedingly dense plumage. Often abroad by day.

VOICE   On breeding grounds displaying males tilt head back and utter strange guttural barks, like a mixture of rooster, raven, and dog, in equal proportions. At nest, female makes purring noises and various clucking sounds; shrill whistles fairly common at nest site, as are hissing and bill clacking.

SIMILAR SPECIES   In pursuit flight snowy owl may be confused with white-phase gyrfalcon, unless huge head is seen; falcon's body much less massive, wings more pointed, tail longer. See barn owl and great horned owl.

RANGE   Circumpolar. In North America, breeds in arctic tundra from Alaska east to Hudson Bay and northern Labrador. Withdraws in winter from high arctic to central prairie region of Canada and northern tier of states in U.S. During irruptive southward flights, birds (mostly young) often reach central states and have turned up as far south as Texas, Louisiana, and Alabama.

HABITAT   Nesting birds favor rolling tundra. Outside breeding area the snowy frequents open situations, such as prairies, marshes, airports, lake shores, and banks of broad rivers. Typically surveys terrain from perches such as fenceposts, haystacks, dunes, chimneys, and rooftops. Seldom found in trees.

NESTING   Nests on ground, in slight depressions thinly lined with grass, feathers, or a little moss. Typically favors high, dry sites; sometimes uses gravel bank or rocky ledge with heavy covering

of lichens. Eggs 4–9, as many as 14 in prey boom periods. Incubation, by female only, 32–34 days. Fledging 50–60 days.

MIGRATION   In North America adult birds regularly migrate south of zone of 24-hour darkness. South-bound irruptions, typically by juveniles, one of most fascinating and complex puzzles of field biology.

PREY   Voles, lemmings, arctic hares, ptarmigans are staple arctic foods. In southward wanderings becomes great opportunist, catching and eating anything it can overpower with relative ease; will not hesitate to pilfer trappers' lines or snatch ducks away from waterfowlers. Theory of close link between owl life cycle and abundance or scarcity of lemmings inaccurate: species has long been successful nester in regions (Iceland, Shetland Islands) with neither lemmings nor lemminglike rodents.

NATURAL HISTORY

Question: What is euphoria? Answer: A birder seeing his first snowy owl . . . or a veteran seeing his fiftieth! No other bird casts such a spell. And none—certainly no other owl—has generated more controversy among biologists trying to unravel the secrets of its nomadic wanderings.

Snowy owls are dramatic, unmistakable, and often easy to approach. In flight years they have been shot, mounted, photographed, or simply looked at and logged in their lists by legions of happy birders. This has created—alas!—a huge mass of data. Now, scientists have the incurable habit of trying to find patterns in any vast stockpile of recorded observations. In the matter of snowy owl flights this has led to learned disputations between investigators who think they see periodicity and those who do not.

An axiom of the periodicists is that snowy owl flights follow regular cycles. Oddly, these are variously held to take place at intervals of

Left: A young-of-the-year female snowy owl perches in tall grass. Below: Snowy owls have a relatively short time in which to hatch their eggs and rear their young before the short arctic summer gives way to the harsh elements of winter.

four, six, seven, or even eleven years. Opponents justly question the worth of such figures. What basis is there for a cycle theory?

Owl flights, say the periodicists, are linked to fluctuations in the numbers of key food animals in the tundra—specifically the two species of arctic lemmings. Trying to solve the riddle of lemming mass migrations has entangled biologists in thickets of speculation, not a few of which lead into the twilight zone. Of all the ideas advanced to explain the baffling behavior of these beasties none is wackier than the theory of a rodent version of the death wish.

According to this bizarre yet widely held notion, genetically built-in sensors tell the lusty little lemmings when their lovemaking has gone too far and their numbers are dangerously overextended. Presto! A special weeding-out instinct comes into play; mass suicide ensues.

If one can believe this, one can also believe that snowy owls have the ability to pick up on the lemmings' intentions. Sensing imminent famine, they not only fly south looking for better hunting grounds, but when they come back they even tailor their egg laying precisely to lemming availability. In springs following really huge lemming crashes, some periodicists tell us, the owls will lay no eggs at all.

None of this is in fact demonstrable. In the first place, snowy owls have bred, probably since time immemorial, in places such as Iceland where neither lemmings nor rodents resembling lemmings have ever been known to exist. Moreover, it has been repeatedly observed that in places where both voles and lemmings are abundant, the owls will show a preference for voles.

Snowies, let's face it, do eat lemmings, often in huge numbers. And lemmings do have four-year cycles. These, however, are neither geographically nor chronologically uniform. Along the immense expanse of the circumpolar tundra, some populations rise while others dwindle and still others remain stable. When and where lemming numbers are low, some snowies will head south for more fertile pastures.

In certain areas—northern coastal New England is an excellent example—the number of these regular winter visitants will be seen to rise appreciably at relatively regular four-year intervals. But it is important to note that of these four-year birds 75 percent are usually juveniles.

By contrast, many adult snowy owls, in North America at least, are regular yearly migrants. Their wintering grounds are the north-central prairies. The environs of Calgary, Alberta, are a favorite foraging area for these birds, only 25 percent of which are immatures.

Thus, both the periodicists and their opponents are, to a degree, correct. Some snowy owls do fly south in response to periodic scarcity of a favorite food, the delectable lemming; these are generally young-of-the-year owls. On the other hand, many other birds, generally adults, head south each winter to spots where there is a little sun and hayricks beckon with the promise of plump and plentiful mice.

This still leaves the problem of the truly phenomenal flights, such as those of 1890 and 1926. During the winters of those years untold thousands of snowies poured down the length and breadth of the U.S. The flood began as early as late October and continued unabated for two and a half months. A fair number of birds even reached the Gulf states. It is shocking to note, even today, the number of these grand, confiding animals that were butchered in cold blood and stuffed to adorn

the mantelpieces of two-legged, featherless raptors far less attractive than they. During the 1926 flight, for instance, more than 150 snowy owls were shot between November and December in the New York City area alone.

The key to these irruptions lies in the biomechanics of the polar regions. Arctic ecology is notoriously unstable; arctic weather shifts can be sudden and murderous. Enormous die-outs of snow geese and musk oxen have been caused by long spells of brutal high-latitude weather.

To killer weather must be added food-related stress. Arctic hares go through eleven-year boom-bust cycles; rock and willow ptarmigans now and then vanish from their usual haunts; and let us not forget the lemmings and their controversial ups and downs.

Whenever protracted blasts of unusually severe weather coincide with a simultaneous crash of these staple foods, a tremendous southbound exodus of snowy owls will follow—to the joy of bird lovers everywhere. No small part of that joy is the knowledge that many of the birds will return to the tundra; thankfully, most of today's hunters use a camera instead of a shotgun.

NORTHERN HAWK OWL
(*Surnia ulula*)

Left: A northern hawk owl perches atop a spruce tree. Right: Typical hawk owl habitat—brushy, scrubby spruce growths.

DESCRIPTION Size 14–17 inches (tail 7 inches); wingspan 31–35 inches. A sleek, day-flying, medium-size "earless" owl with a very long tail and pointed wings. Dark chocolate brown above with white spots; facial disks framed by heavy black "sideburns"; breast and belly creamy white to pale buff, boldly barred crosswise with cinnamon brown. Most hawklike of owls, it flies close to ground like accipiter hawk or large shrike, rising abruptly to its perch (typically tip of tall dead spruce), where it jerks tail upward and lowers it slowly, like kestrel. Diurnal and confiding (not tame!), it allows close approach.

VOICE Like many owls, a versatile and persistent vocalist on and around nesting site, less so elsewhere. Male's nuptial song a melodious, rolling, whistled trill—*ululululululululu* or *tu-roo-roo-roo-roo-roo*—ten seconds long or more "repeated again and again . . . with the same persistence that marks the Whippoorwill's iterations" (R. Clement). Distress call a throaty, rolling rattle, often rising to a penetrating scream—*scrrreee-YIP!, krrreeeEEEP!,* or *krrrrOUK!*—often aimed at intruder approaching nest. Also fairly common are low, raven-like notes—*kuk-a-wuk*—and a rapid *wur-a, wur-a* (or *whir-u, whir-u*), as well as a shrill, kestrellike yipping. Young have shrill, high-pitched hiss—*khweeee!*—like call of broad-winged hawk but rising at end. Most intriguing vocalization is beautiful cadence, resembling slow version of boreal owl mating song, recorded in Sweden in 1966.

SIMILAR SPECIES Boreal owl (similar face pattern) is much smaller, chunky, has no barring below. In hunting flight, hawk owl might be confused with accipiter hawks*. Large head, bigger size, and wedge-shaped tail separate owl from small, tiny-headed, square-tailed sharp-shinned hawk; big-headed, round-tailed Cooper's hawk accidental in owl's range; northern goshawk much bigger, bluish gray.

---

* Accipiters are short-winged, long-tailed, bird-eating hawks. In North America they include the large (bigger than crow) northern goshawk (*Accipiter gentilis*), the medium (crow-size) Cooper's hawk (*A. cooperii*), and the small (blue jay–size) sharp-shinned hawk (*A. striatus*). All are noted for strong, agile flight.

RANGE	Circumpolar. In North America, from northern Alaska (central Brooks Range) east along edge of tree line to Labrador and Newfoundland, south to British Columbia, Alberta, Saskatchewan, northern Minnesota, northern Wisconsin, northern Michigan, central Ontario, southern Quebec, and New Brunswick. Summering birds observed in Idaho and Montana. Typically winters to northern tier of states.
HABITAT	Muskegs (open bogs) in taiga (boreal evergreen forest), tamarack swamps, open woodlands (coniferous or mixed) or woodland edges. Requires high, exposed lookout perch.
NESTING	In hollow stub of dead spruce or birch, old woodpecker holes, natural tree cavity; may use abandoned nests of hawks or crows. Eggs 3–7 (normally 5–6) from early April to early June. Incubation, by female, 25–28 days. Fledging 25–35 days; independence about 11 weeks.
MIGRATION	Like other arctic birds irrupts southward in low prey winters past northern tier of states, rarely wandering as far south as Nebraska, Ohio, Pennsylvania, and New Jersey.
PREY	*Microtus* voles, lemmings, mice, shrews, snowshoe hares, cottontails. Birds include gray jay, ptarmigan, grouse.

NATURAL HISTORY

Aptly named, this most hawklike of owls behaves like an accipiter hawk or a giant shrike. A diurnal hunter, it often hovers like a kestrel, but more typically it plummets from a high perch, skimming close to the ground, wheeling at great speed through the trees, and then abruptly swooping upward to another perch. Indeed, one of its most remarkable habits is sitting at an angle, in the open, on the tip of a tree (usually a dead spruce or larch), fencepost, or bush while jerking its tail upward and lowering it slowly (a typical kestrel trait), looking for all the world like a neckless, fat-headed falcon. All the while, it fearlessly surveys the world around it, which the hawk owl clearly regards as its private preserve. As cocky as it is confiding, it allows a close approach.

Note, please, that hawk owls are *not* tame (as a dozen or more books would have you believe). Get close enough to a nest to make them fret about their young and they will tear you apart in a trice (as more than a dozen birders have found out to their dismay).

Hawk owls are circumpolar. They live in the belt of coniferous forest (called the taiga) that circles most of the northern hemisphere. The boggy openings called muskegs are their special bailiwick; they are also common in clearings fringing spruce swamps at the bottom of low ridges and can be found at the edges of pastures where field meets forest.

Hawk owls stage irruptive wanderings from time to time. Some of these are dramatic. In trying to provide an explanation for these meanderings we face much the same problem presented by wayfaring snowy owls.

Arctic ecosystems are notoriously unstable. Prey animals, such as lemmings, go through boom-bust cycles that sometimes exhibit periodicity, sometimes not. The numbers of *Microtus* voles (a key hawk owl food) in any given area are especially subject to huge, erratic fluctuations. Being versatile, hawk owls can switch from voles to showshoe hares, or from hares to shrews and birds like gray jays. Nevertheless, in seasons when voles, lemmings, and hares crash simultaneously they must wander widely or starve. It is on such occasions that the great southward flights take place.

Note on Evolution

First described by Linnaeus in the eighteenth century, the hawk owl was reclassified in 1806 by the French biologist Duméril. He made it the single species of a genus for which he invented the name *Surnia*. Latter-day experts chose to rank *Surnia* between *Nyctea* (the snowy owl) and *Glaucidium* (the pygmy owls).

However, the hawk owl may have entered the world as a new species much later than this classification suggests. To the author it looks overwhelmingly like an offshoot of the boreal owl. Boreal owls belong to the genus *Aegolius*. This is held to be the latest group of owls to have evolved. Thus, if my surmise is correct, the northern hawk owl may well be the newest owl of all.

Here are the facts. Arctic and subarctic ecosystems are very recent. They arose after the retreat of the glaciers. Within this new life zone opportunities for fast-flying diurnal birds

Two hawk owl fledglings perch on a spruce branch.

of prey abounded in the muskegs of the so-called spruce-moose biome. The boreal owl had long been the typical (i.e., nocturnal, hearing-dependent) small owl of the muskegs. Its ancestry is proved beyond doubt by fossil remains from preglacial times. But nature, as we know, abhors a vacuum. So let's imagine an evolutionary scenario.

Start with a boreal owl. First, stretch its body out a bit, so it doesn't look like a fat, feathered egg (a hawk owl, after all, must be aerodynamic). While you're at it, give its tail a tug or two—a nice rudder comes in handy for flitting into and around thick stands of spruce. The wings should also be stretched a little, and making the ends pointed (swallowlike) wouldn't hurt, either. Now stiffen up the feathers (no need now for silent flight, but power on the downstroke is important). As a final touch add a pattern of dark crossbars on breast and belly (ideal for countershading—all woodland hawks have similar undersides), and —presto!—the evolutionary miracle has taken place: the boreal owl has been transmogrified into a hawk owl!

Support for this theory comes from the field work of Swedish bioacoustician Sture Palmér. Famous for his recordings of European bird songs, in 1966 Palmér recorded a hawk owl song in his native Sweden that is most suggestive. It is a series of hauntingly beautiful musical whistles, with a distinct liquid quality, delivered in a languid, leisurely rhythm. What is particularly startling about this song is that it is virtually identical to the love song of the boreal owl, slowed down.

Also buttressing this idea is the classification of the owls proposed by N. L. Ford. See page 16 for details.

Two hawk owlets peer from their nesting cavity in the hollow stump of a dead tree.

NORTHERN PYGMY OWL
(*Glaucidium gnoma*)

Left: An adult northern pygmy owl perches on a cedar branch. Right: Typical northern pygmy owl habitat—dense alpine forests of pine or scattered trees.

DESCRIPTION Size 7–7½ inches; wingspan 14½–16 inches. A bold, "earless," long-tailed little owl with a shrikelike flight, often abroad by day. Tail dark brown with six or seven white crossbars, often cocked at perky angle. Upper parts grayish brown or rusty brown; lower breast and belly white, with sharp, dark brown or blackish streaks. Crown and nape profusely stippled with small white dots; scapulars and wings have rows of larger, buff-white spots. Eyes yellow. Nape has large, black, oval false eyespots, rimmed with white, making owl look double faced—a pygmy owl hallmark; helps ward off predators.

VOICE Primary call an evenly paced, single or double, clear whistled tooting, with considerable geographical and seasonal variation—*too-too-too* (leisurely rhythm, typical of northern birds) or *too-too, too-too, too-too* (fast rhythm, typical of southern birds). Tone varies from bright and silvery to soft and mellow; at times may actually sound hollow and fairly flat; emphasis on resemblance to cooing doves misleading. Most often heard in early morning and late afternoon. Mating birds sing slow, mellow trills, with pause at end followed by two or three longer notes.

SIMILAR SPECIES Very similar ferruginous pygmy owl has reddish tail with dusky crossbars, crown usually streaked (not stippled), different voice. Diurnal habits, tiny size, smallish head, long, white-barred tail, and sharply streaked underparts separate this species visually from larger, dome-headed, short-tailed, thickly banded, typically nocturnal saw-whet owl. Vocally the birds might be confused: saw-whet song usually less pulsing, flatter, more monotonous; usually given later at night. Nevertheless, there is overlap both in tone and time of delivery; novices should be cautious in distinguishing these two owls by voice.

RANGE From southeastern Alaska and British Columbia south along Pacific coast to southern California; east to western Alberta and south to Rockies throughout western states, continuing, in higher mountains of Mexico, to Guatemala and Honduras.

HABITAT	Open coniferous forests; open oak, pine-oak, and streambank woodlands. Favors glades, tree-girded alpine meadows, forest edges, and other open spots with nearby trees. Found up to 10,000 feet.
NESTING	Typically uses abandoned holes excavated by flickers, acorn woodpeckers, or hairy woodpeckers; also natural tree cavities. Eggs 2–7, usually 3–4, from April through June. Incubation, by female, 28 days; owlets leave nest in about one month.
MIGRATION	Essentially sedentary. Some withdrawal from higher mountain haunts during severe winter weather.
PREY	Chipmunks, mice, ground squirrels, large insects, small reptiles, and amphibians. Becomes active bird hunter with owlets in nest; takes almost any species of bird it can overpower with relative ease.

Top left: A northern pygmy owl perches on a tree branch. Once found, the northern pygmy is quite tame and easily approached. Left: Pygmy owls show dark spots on the nape—false "eyes" that discourage other birds from harassing or molesting the tiny owls from behind. Above: A pygmy owl peers out of its nest fifty feet above the ground in a ponderosa pine in California.

NATURAL HISTORY

The northern pygmy owl is a diminutive raptor found in the giant conifers of the Pacific slope as well as in open pine-oak woodlands and riparian forests. Since it often hunts during the day it is much easier to see than other owls that share its habitat.

Pygmy owls are feathered fireballs. Ounce for ounce no other predator in their territory can match them for pugnacity and fearlessness. They have been known to tackle blue grouse, almost twenty times their weight. Ground squirrels, chipmunks, chickarees (the western counterpart of the red squirrel), and many species of montane birds are frequent victims of this tiny avian hunter. The list of

songbirds known to have been taken by pygmy owls reads like a checklist from a western field guide.

A reckless butcher, however, the northern pygmy owl is not. Only when their chicks are hungry do parent pygmy owls prey on warblers, thrushes, and wrens. When not burdened with young, they are content to munch on mice, crickets, and an occasional moth. The birds of the forest do not appreciate such fine distinctions, however. No self-respecting nuthatch, titmouse, oriole, or jay will miss a chance to vent its spleen on any pygmy owl—Public Enemy Number One—unlucky enough to be caught napping in the open.

Indeed, being harried by mobs of angry birds is a routine feature in the life of this owl, and its knack for arousing the wrath of just about every species of nesting songbird in the West has made it a boon to bird census takers. Imitate a pygmy owl call or play its song on a tape recorder and you can confidently expect a flying phalanx of bushtits, chickadees, kinglets, wrens, warblers, woodpeckers, finches, orioles, and jays to pop out of thickets you would have sworn harbored not a single bird!

A fascinating behavioral feature of this species is that it seldom emerges from cover at night. The same is true of the ferruginous pygmy owl. Staying put in a cavity or in dense cover is how pygmies avoid being eaten by larger, more powerful owls, as well as by weasels and other four-legged carnivores. With daybreak the owl springs into action. Time for breakfast. Time, also, to "keep at bay the hawk that hunts by day," not to mention such other nasty neighbors as sharp-beaked jays, ever ready to spoil the pleasure of eating the first mouse of the morning.

It is then that the owl's eyespots come into play. The necks of owls are amazingly flexible, but owl eyes are fixed in their sockets; so the birds need to rotate their heads to catch sight of food or foe. They often seem to turn their heads in a complete circle and at spectacular speed. But a perched pygmy can scan for voles with total peace of mind: if it flips its face to the north to check out a rustle in the grass, it knows that a Cooper's hawk coming from the south will find itself staring at two enormous black eyes framed by not two but four fearsome white eyebrows.

When hunting by day the pygmy owl suggests a stubby, bull-necked shrike. This is especially true when it dashes about clearings or forest edges. In the heart of the tall woods it often flies high above the ground, deftly and quickly skirting the big trees, looking for all the world like a little, fat accipiter hawk. The din raised on such occasions by Steller's jays and assorted forest rodents is unforgettable.

In line with its shrikelike behavior this owl will sometimes glide low over the ground and swoop up to a post, where it will perch, scanning the surroundings with goggles that seldom miss a worthwhile morsel. While thus engaged, pygmy owls will gaze intently at anything that moves. Hikers will get as much attention as shrews. On the Hoh River Trail in the Olympic Peninsula a pygmy owl once sat on the tip of a twelve-foot trail marker and calmly counted hikers for ten minutes.

A northern pygmy owl fluffs its feathers to retain warmth while hunting in a western forest.

FERRUGINOUS PYGMY OWL
(*Glaucidium brasilianum*)

Left: A ferruginous pygmy owl perches on a branch with its prey, a mouse. This mainly diurnal owl is most active at dawn and dusk, and subsists on insects along with mice. Right: A juvenile ferruginous pygmy owl in its nest cavity prior to fledging.

DESCRIPTION   Identical in size and shape to northern pygmy owl. Also has a gray-brown and a rusty form; Arizona birds often distinctly pale gray. Key fieldmark is tail, which is always rusty, with 7–8 dark crossbars; some birds have uniformly dark tails. In many birds top of head is finely streaked (not stippled) with white. Largely diurnal; sings, but seldom flies, on moonlit nights.

VOICE   Primary song distinctive and diagnostic: a fast-paced series of short, sharp, throaty, pulsating whistles, with a distinct "popping" quality, delivered at a snappy rhythm (as many as 2–3 per second)—*khuit-khuit-khuit, pruik-pruik-pruik,* or *poip-poip-poip*—from 10–60 whistles per series. Call much more rapid and explosive than sequence of musical whistles of northern pygmy owl. Ferruginous pygmy owls have been heard uttering many other vocalizations, some remarkably complex.

SIMILAR SPECIES   See northern pygmy owl. Only small owl likely to be found in ferruginous habitat in latter's U.S. range is tiny, dark, short-tailed elf owl—a species that lacks eyespots on nape and flies only at night (ferruginous owl almost never does).

RANGE   Very rare and local in south-central Arizona and lower Rio Grande Valley; has occurred in southwestern New Mexico. Widely distributed south of the border, from Mexico to Brazil, with a separate population in southern South America.

HABITAT   Mesquite thickets, saguaro cactus desert, thorn scrub, cottonwoods along riverbanks.

NESTING   Woodpecker holes in cottonwoods, saguaro cactus, or mesquite; natural tree cavities. Eggs 3–5, from March to early June. Incubation, by female, 28 days; owlets fly 27–30 days after hatching.

MIGRATION   Winter displacement poorly known. Birds at northern extreme of range almost certainly move southward during especially severe cold spells.

PREY   Crickets and other large insects, caterpillars, scorpions; lizards and other reptiles; wide variety of desert songbirds; small rodents.

NATURAL HISTORY

This species replaces the northern pygmy owl in desert areas with dense growths of mesquite, cholla, and saguaro. Less frequently it occurs in riparian woodlands, especially cottonwood stands. Major Charles Bendire, in his classic *Life Histories of North American Birds* (1892), cites the Gila and Salt River valleys in southeastern Arizona as areas once frequented by this owl. As any observer of urban sprawl will ruefully attest, many of the choicest wooded tracts along these and other southwestern river valleys are now shopping malls. This, and other stress factors that are far less clear, have brought about a calamitous plunge in the population of ferruginous pygmy owls north of the Mexican border. Its numbers do not seem to have shrunk appreciably from northern Mexico south to Brazil, and a separate population thrives in the Patagonian region of Argentina.

Like its northern cousin this spunky little owl is a fearless hunter. It will take on mammals twice its size and pounce on birds as big as thrashers. Fast and nimble on the wing, it goes after and actually catches hummingbirds. Hummingbirds, in turn, obviously relish getting even. Let a ferruginous pygmy owl be unfortunate enough to be detected by these minispitfires and the strafing and dive bombing that ensues will put any Rickenbacker or Red Baron to shame.

Augusto Ruschi, the great hummingbird expert, put this capacity of the ferruginous pygmy owl to incite hummingbirds to excellent use. Whenever he wanted to capture a live hummer he would tether a ferruginous pygmy owl to a pole planted in the ground and wait. Provided there were hummingbirds in the area, he was never disappointed.

Left: Three ferruginous pygmy owlets exhibit branching behavior.
Above left: An adult ferruginous pygmy owl reveals false "eyes" on the back of its head.
Above right: The same bird demonstrates its ability to rotate its head 180 degrees. With a name that means "rust-colored," one of its prominent characteristics is a red, faintly crossed and barred tail.

ELF OWL
(*Micrathene whitneyi*)

Left: A fledgling elf owl perches on cactus at sunset. The elf owl can often be located at night by its high-pitched, tremulous voice consisting of varied whistles and whinnies. Right: Typical elf owl habitat—desert terrain with cactus and brush. Elf owls are commonly found in canyons and desert lowlands, especially in oaks and sycamores, and nest in cavities in saguaro cacti or trees.

DESCRIPTION Size 5–6 inches; wingspan 14–15 inches. Smallest owl in North America, size of small sparrow. Tuftless, with a very short tail and brilliant yellow eyes, highlighted by black outer rim and white "eyebrows." Facial disks pale fox red or reddish buff. Gray-brown above with buff spots on back, white spots on shoulders; off-white below with blurry buff-brown stripes. Hides by day in hole in cactus or tree or deepest part of thicket. Seldom seen before dusk.

VOICE Remarkably varied; J. D. Ligon has described at least a dozen calls. Most often heard is rapid high-pitched series of 6 or more yips or cackling chirps—*whi-whi-whi-whi-whi-whi, chewk-chewk-chewk,* or *tyew-tyew-tyew*—typically rising in pitch and becoming more chattering, yippy, and puppylike in the middle; sung as duet by male and female. Given at night, call is best cue to presence of bird.

SIMILAR SPECIES Ferruginous and northern pygmy owls chiefly diurnal; have long tails, black "eyes" on hind neck, sharp stripes on flanks and belly. Screech and whiskered owls larger, grayer, tufted. Dark-eyed flammulated owl usually in higher terrain, different habitat. See also saw-whet owl.

RANGE Extremely rare in southeast California (reintroduction efforts may restore former abundance); common in central and southern Arizona; fairly common in southwest New Mexico; rare and declining in southern Texas. Nests south to Puebla and Guanajuato. Winters south to Río Balsas basin, Mexico.

HABITAT Deserts, especially saguaro stands; sycamores and cottonwoods along streams; oak and pine-oak woodlands in foothills and lower slopes of canyons; dense thickets. Favors elevations of 3,000–5,000 feet; has been found as high as 7,000 feet.

NESTING Holes in saguaros excavated by Gila woodpecker or gilded flicker or in oaks, pines, sycamores, cottonwoods excavated by same and by Strickland's, golden-fronted, and acorn woodpeckers;

Below: An adult elf owl with a moth in its beak flies back to nest. The elf owl is mainly a nocturnal hunter. Top above right: An adult elf owl arrives at its nest in a saguaro cactus with insect in beak. Below right: A fledgling juvenile perches amid the blossoms of a saguaro.

also natural tree cavities. Eggs 2–4, from late March to June. Female incubates clutch 24 days; young leave nest in 28–32 days.

<table>
<tr><td>MIGRATION</td><td>Northern birds highly migratory; almost all U.S. nesters fly south abruptly in late October. Northward migration, equally abrupt, from late February to mid-March.</td></tr>
<tr><td>PREY</td><td>Catches beetles, hawk moths, grasshoppers, and crickets on wing and on the ground; takes spiders, vinegarroons, and scorpions (removes sting before eating); small reptiles round out diet. Attracted to camp lights and cactus blooms.</td></tr>
</table>

NATURAL HISTORY

Mention of this minuscule owl conjures up visions of Joseph Wood Krutch's beloved Sonoran Desert: cactus wrens, kangaroo rats, roadrunners, coyotes, mesquite thickets, and—towering over all—the improbable and extraordinary giant saguaros. Considering that hundreds of these delightful, bright-eyed mites have been painted or photographed peering out of a saguaro, the association between them and this colossus of the cactus tribe is almost automatic.

Elf owls are nocturnal. By moonlight, they hunt scorpions, moths, and other arthropods in areas where at dawn and dusk pygmy owls go on the prowl. To avoid attack by these

"dynamite sticks with wings" a safe roosting site is clearly a top priority. For this the elf owl may take advantage of the dense cover of a streamside thicket or use woodpecker holes and natural tree cavities. In any case, the cavities earmarked for nesting are seldom used as hideouts. Thus, "elves," which are prolific, exert intense pressure on a limited resource in their search for thickets and cavities in desert vegetation.

Elves that nest in saguaros use holes dug out by Gila woodpeckers or gilded flickers. When these chisel-billed birds scoop out their holes in the cactus, the plant secretes a slushy liquid that dries up hard, creating a tough and

Left: An elf owl fledgling perches on a prickly pear cactus blossom. Above: A young elf owl at the entrance to its nesting cavity in a saguaro cactus.

durable inner wall. The cavities stay cool during the heat of the day, but after sunset they are warmer than the often chilly desert nights. Thus they make ideal homes for elf owls as well as woodpeckers.

Much as an elf owl might prefer a studio in a saguaro to a condo in a conifer, there aren't enough of the giant cacti to meet the housing needs of this prolific species. J. D. Ligon, Joe Marshall, and Lew Walker have shown elf owls to be in abundance on the lower slopes of Arizona canyon lands. There, in cavities in pines, sycamores, cottonwoods, and oaks, the elves take refuge from the heat and hungry pygmy owls and bring up their babies.

Elf owls eat arthropods. But spiders, scorpions, and bugs are killed off or driven underground by the cold. Thus the owls that nest in the north must fly south for food in winter. Since these northern nesters are already close to the hotter parts of Mexico, the southbound exodus is massive and brief. Much the same happens when the owls move north in spring as the desert warms up. Toward the end of February a few trickle through. Later hundreds mass together at traditional border crossings; then quite suddenly in March, the moonlit air of the Sonoran Desert is again alive with the love calls of these engaging Lilliputians of the owl tribe.

BURROWING OWL
(*Athene cunicularia*)

Left: Adult burrowing owls perch on a fence-post near their den, using the post as a platform to watch for danger. Right: Typical burrowing owl habitat—open sage-brush country.

DESCRIPTION
Size 8½–11 inches; wingspan 20–24 inches. A small, light tan, long-legged owl with a stubby tail. Often seen by daylight standing on ground next to burrow or on fencepost in open country. When excited bows deeply and bobs up and down on stiltlike legs. Flight strongly undulating. Top of head, back, and wings sandy colored; bright white "eyebrows" above flattish facial disks; dark collar separates white throat bib from white band on upper breast; rest of underparts whitish with light brown bars. Females larger and darker. Juveniles buff, with no bars below.

VOICE
Alarm call a sharp, chattering *cack-cack-cack* or *quick-quick-quick,* given by both sexes on ground and in flight. Primary song, repeatedly given at night by courting males, a clear, emphatic *coo-coooo! coo-coooo!* or *coo-coo-rooo! coo-coo-rooo!,* not unlike cooing dove but higher pitched and delivered at smart pace, like song of Old World cuckoo. Other calls a sharp *chuck!,* a scream followed by series of chattering notes. From inside burrow disturbed owlets utter sound that closely mimics buzzing of large rattlesnake.

SIMILAR SPECIES
Shape, behavior, and habitat make this owl unique and unmistakable.

RANGE
Western race ranges from southern British Columbia east to south-central Manitoba and eastern edge of Great Plains (Minnesota), then south along broad belt (Pacific, western, and central states) to Baja California (including offshore islands) in west, Texas and Louisiana in east; also broadly distributed in Mexico, Central America, and South America. Eastern race, formerly found only in Cuba and prairies of southern and central Florida, extending range northward, chiefly in response to manmade open spaces.

HABITAT
Prairies, semiarid desert plains, other open grasslands; barren plateaus; high sandy islands; margins of airports and golf courses; railroad rights-of-way, road shoulders, canal dykes; vacant urban lots. Found from 200 feet below sea level (Death Valley, California) to 9,000 feet above (Colorado plateaus).

NESTING   Underground, in small colonies. Can dig own burrow but prefers deserted excavations of prairie dogs in west, of armadillos and gopher tortoises in east; uses abandoned burrows of badgers, ground squirrels, woodchucks, and skunks; rarely, deserted dens of foxes, coyotes, wolves. Often lines nest with dry, shredded horse or cow manure, dry leaves, wide assortment of other litter; mound at mouth of burrow serves as lookout for parents. Undisturbed owls use same nest year after year. Eggs 6–11, usually 7–9, from March to July. Incubation, by both sexes, 3–4 weeks.

MIGRATION   Partly migratory: northernmost birds move south in severe winters; downslope displacement typical of owls in high mountain habitats. Accidental in Great Lakes region, New England, and the Carolinas.

PREY   Insects, especially locusts and crickets; also moths, beetles, dragonflies (often caught in flight); other arthropods, including scorpions, centipedes, crayfish. Small mammals, especially mice, gophers, ground squirrels, and rats; also takes young cottontails, bats, and shrews; frogs and toads, salamanders, lizards, snakes; rarely, small birds, such as sparrows and horned larks.

NATURAL HISTORY

In many areas of the New World this perky little extrovert is often the bird finder's first owl. Indeed, it is readily recognized as an owl, and much liked for its beneficial eating habits by ranchers and farmers, who have affectionately dubbed it "billy owl" and "howdy-do owl."

The latter nickname refers to the owl's habit of bowing to the ground and bobbing up and down on legs that look like sparsely feathered stilts. Courtesy is hardly the bird's intention; the movement, in fact, expresses agitation. After all, it is directed toward a gigantic two-legged intruder who doesn't even have feathers! Let the monster come closer and the billy owl will either dive into its cellarette or strafe the unwelcome biped, stridently voicing its displeasure.

Left and above: Young burrowing owls near the entrance to their den.

Prairie dogs and burrowing owls go together like the proverbial horse and buggy. The owls do not share burrows with the rodents—in fact, they favor towns that prairie dogs have abandoned—but they are often seen in each other's company. Not infrequently a common enemy like the ferruginous hawk will startle a prairie dog and a burrowing owl into leaping together into the same hole. The prairie rattlesnake haunts prairie dog towns. A zoo collector once caught three hundred of these vipers in three days within a quarter-mile radius of one colony. As he left the colony at the end of each day the collector noted that owls and "dogs" would come to the surface again. Interestingly, burrowing owls can mimic the prairie rattler's buzz just about perfectly. Owlets inside a burrow use this talent to scare off predators.

However, the old wives' tale that owl, rodent, and snake share underground digs as one big, happy family is sheer nonsense. Burrowing owls eat baby prairie dogs, and the rattlers eat both prairie dogs and burrowing owls. What brings the animals together is a slowly evolved, closely knit interdependence. Arguably, some degree of resource-sharing takes place among them, but the friendship is nothing more than folklore.

A similar myth prevails in Florida regarding the diamondback rattlesnake, the owl, and the gopher tortoise. Burrows dug by the tortoise are used by the snake and the owl. Diamondbacks, fearsome as they are, are not much of a threat to the tortoise, but they will readily kill and eat a family of owls. A diamondback crawling out of a burrow that hours earlier sported a pair of howdy-do owls generally means that the birds (and almost certainly their eggs) have been supped on by the snake.

Burrowing owls are "barometer birds." In fact few animals illustrate more clearly how development both helps and hinders the well-being of species. Prairie dog towns have been destroyed on a vast scale. This has led to the disappearance not only of owls, but of a whole web of wildlife intimately linked to these rodent communities: prairie rattlesnakes, foxes, coyotes, ferruginous hawks, and black-footed ferrets. Only in a few isolated preserves can one still observe the primeval prey-predator interactions once evident in numerous prairie dog cities.

But the owls have learned to survive by taking advantage of airports, golf courses, and dykes along ditches, not to mention highway shoulders, landfills, and vacant lots in and around urban centers.

Above: A juvenile burrowing owl begs food from an adult. Right: An adult burrowing owl on sagebrush, adjacent to its den entrance.

A few years back the owls began nesting along the runways of the Miami airport, and special carts were provided to tote tourists to their windswept burrows. In Cape Coral the owls set up housekeeping in a lot flanked by the post office, a supermarket, and a real estate office. On a busy Saturday, moms, tots, dogs (on leash and off), businessmen, bird watchers, and several pairs of burrowing owls with pesky full-grown babes—all scurrying about in the fulfillment of their appointed rounds—created a spectacle not easily forgotten.

Note on Evolution

Just as the northern hawk owl might be the most recent of all owls, the burrowing owl may turn out to be one of the first members of the tribe to have jelled in the pressure cooker of evolution. A fossil ankle and upper foot of great antiquity has recently been determined to have belonged to an owl—presumably long extinct. However, a comparison of this fossil with the ankle/foot of a burrowing owl shows the bones to be almost identical. So close is the resemblance, in fact, that it is not far-fetched to think that burrowing owls, or birds very much like them, roamed the American prairies when there were still dinosaurs around. See pages 15–16 for details.

BARRED OWL
(*Strix varia*)

Left: A barred owlet perches atop an old cedar stump in Washington state. It had fledged its nest just the night before. Right: Typical barred owl habitat—dense deciduous forest. Barred owls inhabit mixed woods of river bottoms or swamps and dense deciduous or coniferous forests. During the winter, these owls may be found in upland woods.

DESCRIPTION
Size 16–24 inches; wingspan 38–50 inches. A large, rotund, gray-brown woodland owl with a puffy dome-shaped head and big, liquid black eyes*. Most striking feature is ruff of feathers, barred crosswise, on puffy upper breast, bold lengthwise streaks on rest of underparts. Amount and richness of brown in plumage increases from north to south: palest birds (little or no trace of brown) in east-central Canada (Quebec race); darkest (rusty brown race *fulvescens†*) in extreme south Mexico and adjacent Central America; some pale individuals also in Texas.

VOICE
Most vocal of owls; often called the "eight-hooter." Best known call two groups of four hoots each, vigorously rhythmic, emphatically delivered—*howWHO-haWHOO! ... howWHO-haWHOOAaahh!* (often represented as "*Who-cooks-for-you? Who-cooks-for-you-all?*"). Tonal quality unique: blend of bark and hoot with touch of nausea at end. Vast repertoire includes lengthy contrapuntal duets; sharp ascending whistle—*shoeeet!* (young; brooding female); deep gurgling territorial defense song (male); amazing variety of wails, moans, cackles, hisses, and laughs. For good measure they are quite capable of long, loud, unnervingly humanlike screams. Often call by day, especially before thunderstorms.

SIMILAR SPECIES
Very similar spotted owl darker, has white spots on head and back, lacks contrast between barred breast and streaked belly; song simpler, usually less emphatic. Great gray owl and first-year female snowy owl (both have yellow eyes) may be confused with pale northern barred owls.

RANGE
From British Columbia and Alberta east to central Quebec and Nova Scotia south throughout eastern United States (east of 100th meridian) to Gulf Coast, including Florida and Texas. Dramatic expansion in West; now resident in Washington, western Montana, Oregon, western

---

* Eye color source of much confusion—at distance iris looks brown; at close range proves to be a strange blue-black.

† This form is treated as a full species, the fulvous owl *S. fulvescens*, in the sixth edition of the American Ornithologists' Union's *Checklist of North American Birds* (1983).

Idaho, and northern California. Also in central and eastern Mexico south to Oaxaca and Veracruz; "red" birds (*fulvescens*) in cloud forests of Chiapas (southern Mexico), Guatemala, Honduras, and El Salvador.

HABITAT Woodland swamps, dense forests; lakeshores, river bottomlands, ravines; does not shun drier high country provided big trees present; found in mixed, evergreen, and deciduous woodland. Especially numerous in cypress swamps of Southeast.

NESTING Cavities in trees; abandoned nests of crows, ravens, hawks, especially red-shouldered hawk (evidence of communal nesting); presence of big trees key factor. Remarkable site fidelity: one pair returned to same nest for 33 years. Open stump nests very rare (contra some authorities). Eggs 2–4, usually 2, January (Florida) to June (Texas), usually late February to late May. Incubation, mostly by female, 28–32 days; fledging 40–45 days.

MIGRATION Sedentary. Occasional massive displacements (generally from inland areas toward seashore) during very severe cold spells.

PREY Many kinds of mice, woodrats, chipmunks, squirrels, opossums, shrews. Wide variety of insects, especially large beetles and crickets, noctuid moths. Takes snakes, lizards, salamanders, crayfish, frogs; wades in shallow water for fish. Also birds like quail, grouse, doves, flickers, jays, finches; known to eat smaller owls and bats.

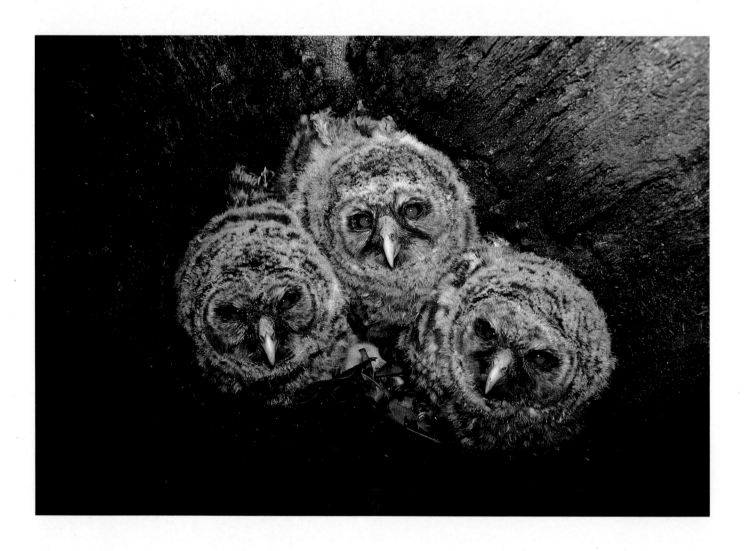

Left: Three barred owlets in an old-growth nesting cavity. Above: An adult barred owl in the Florida Everglades.

NATURAL HISTORY

Barred owls are marvelous birds: they are the champion vocalists of the tribe; they have engaging personalities; and they are beautifully marked. Mary Durant, in *On the Road with John James Audubon,* says: "Visually the barred owl is, to me, the most elegant of its tribe. Seen from the front, it wears a brown and white muffler slung loosely across its throat, and below the muffler a loose gown of the same brown and white pattern."

The barred owl is the nocturnal counterpart of the red-shouldered hawk. Both birds are at home in moist bottomland woodlands. Frogs, crawfish, and water snakes are avidly eaten by both species. In contrast with great horned owls, which have been known forcibly to dislodge red-tailed hawks from their nests and even to kill them, barred owls and red-shouldered hawks live on fairly peaceable terms. Thus the owl and the hawk that typify aerial predation in wooded swamps not only agree in their choice of food and real estate, but may even now and then share a nesting site.

The benign nature of the barred owl is attested by myriad observers. In this respect it is the opposite number of the great horned owl. Great horned owls are majestic, aloof, and dangerous. Barred owls are quite harmless and try to appear horrifying. At this they do a first-rate job. What the bird lacks in genuine ferocity it more than makes up in acting ability. A barred owl will glide directly toward a birder's eyes, break flight seconds before contact, and perch a few feet away, glowering menacingly. From this position of disquieting intimacy, it will swell its neck, puff out its chest, crane its head, and distend its already bulging eyes so that it looks like an enormous goitered Toby Jug. Then, to cap off the performance, it will take a deep breath and pour out a torrent of strixine obscenities guaranteed to unhinge the most placid soul. Its concert of wails, cackles, and barks, often punctuated with gurgles, chuckles, and maniacal laughter, is sure to startle the first-time observer when delivered in broad daylight. But at night the performance is spine-chilling, even to the strix-

ine addict of long standing. This is particularly true when the barred owl chooses to put on one of its finest—and mercifully rare—vocal acts: starting out from a complete standstill, bioacoustically speaking, the barred owl will utter a long, loud, blood-curdling scream that sounds as if a human were being skewered with a red-hot iron.

The ethological significance of this call has thus far eluded all who have heard it—possibly because their attention at the moment has been fixed on running away (or recovering the ability to run away), leaving no time to decipher the meaning of the sound in the context of barred owl semantics.

The barred owl's unforeseeable and spectacular colonization of the Northwest has brought some essential facets of evolutionary dynamics into sharp focus. This is because in its takeover it has invaded the haunts of a close relative, the spotted owl.

This last species is an engaging but baffling bird. In many ways it is so like the barred owl that some taxonomists have preferred to consider it merely a race, or subspecies, of that bird—a view that the interactions of both species, now that they have apparently met for the first time, just do not seem to uphold.

These interactions, and their implications, will be explored in detail in the next owl portrait.

Above: An adult barred owl. Right: An adult barred owl perches on an alder branch. These mainly nocturnal owls can become active during the day, when a heavy forest canopy and thick cloud cover combine to darken their habitat.

SPOTTED OWL
(Strix occidentalis)

Left: A spotted owl perches on a tree branch. Right: An adult northern spotted owl roosts amid old-growth trees in Mount Rainier National Park in Washington state.

DESCRIPTION   Size 16–19 inches; wingspan 42–45 inches. A rare western counterpart of the barred owl; large, dark, dome-headed, black-eyed, with a profusion of white spots on head and back; underparts show a uniform pattern of rectangular brown and white bars, lack barred owl's contrast between barred throat and striped belly. Extremely confiding; allows close approach.

VOICE   Like barred owl but more subdued. Four major vocalizations: series of 3–4 hoots (males, deep, mellow; females, high, penetrating)—*who-who . . . WHOOo; whup . . . who-who . . . WHOOo.* or *who . . . huWHO . . . whoOOo*—leisurely pace, last note longer, accented; series of yelps at even pitch and pace, accelerating slightly, ending with longer, louder notes—*ho-ho-ho-ho-ho-ho-ha-ha-haHOOah-haHOOah-HOOah!*—very doglike, may be confused with call of coyote; sharp rising whistle with snap at end—*shoeeEEE'yip!*—like that of barred owl but more frequent (females, young); duet version of last two (male yelps, female whistles). Many other calls, some soft, others explosive.

SIMILAR SPECIES   See barred owl. Only other dark-eyed owls in range are barn (distinctive, different habitat) and flammulated (tiny, tufted).

RANGE   Discontinuous. Resident in dense forests of Pacific slope from southern British Columbia south to San Francisco Bay; in western slope of Sierra Nevada to south-central California; in highlands of southwestern California from Santa Barbara to San Diego; in southern Rocky Mountains from central Colorado south through Arizona and New Mexico into west-central Mexico.

HABITAT   Dense montane forests, mostly coniferous; requires groves of mature trees (Douglas fir, Ponderosa pine, redwoods); ravines, forested canyons. Typically close to permanently running water.

NESTING   Crevices, potholes, and caves in canyons and cliffs; abandoned nests of crows, ravens, or hawks (including red-tailed and Cooper's); cavities in trees; stump ends of sycamores, oaks. Eggs 2–4

(high number very rare; usually 2), from early March to early May. Incubation, by female, about 1 month. Young drop out of nest when 5 weeks old, fly at 6 weeks.

MIGRATION   None. Some altitudinal displacement in winter.

PREY   Flying squirrels, woodrats, tree mice (*Phenacomys*), white-footed mice, et cetera; crickets, large beetles, owlet moths; birds like Steller's jays, smaller owls, and bats. Has been lured to feeding stations.

NATURAL HISTORY

The spotted owl is a close relative of the barred owl. Some experts, in fact, treat the spotted as a subspecies, or race, of the barred. Without going quite so far, it can be argued that in some ways the spotted is an attenuated version of its more widespread and aggressive eastern counterpart. This comes out clearly in the bird's calls: the courtship song of a male "spotty" sounds like a shorter and less energetic version of the equivalent call of the barred owl.

Spotties are nonetheless unique.

They share with the barred a passion for the forest primeval, but theirs is an even more intense attachment to the giant trees. For the spotted owl has become specialized to life in mature stands of Ponderosa pines, redwoods,

Douglas firs, and the other colossal conifers of the Cascades. It does not disdain other western mountain chains with dense groves of evergreens, and it is found in pine-oak associations in southwestern canyons. In all three biotopes the bird is rare and local. In the canyon lands it is, if anything, more restricted than in the moist mountain slopes of the Northwest, where an occasional unbroken tract of spruce or fir affords a fair chance for growing owlets to fan out and find new nesting sites.

Canyon-dwelling spotted owls tend to favor isolated localities, mostly close to caves and crevices that offer shelter and a safe spot for a nest; typically, these sites are seldom far from water. Clear running water is in fact such a powerful attractant to these birds (who are fond of bathing) that one can almost predict a nearby stream wherever a spotty is heard hooting. Conversely, an evergreen-clad gorge with a gurgling brook is just the place to look for this beautiful and astonishingly sweet-tempered bird.

Many canyon-land caves have long histories of continuous occupation. Not surprisingly they have correspondingly long histories of heavy use by birders intent on ticking off this species on their life lists.

---

* See also Chapter 9, Conservation.

Paradoxically, this has become easier now that the owl has been declared a threatened species.* Legions of volunteers comb the woods on the alert for its doglike duets; eco-tacticians lose sleep over critical habitat threatened by loggers; and field biologists fret about competition from the barred owl.

As the barred owls have moved west, like gold-rush prospectors, the specter of displacement from its stakeouts has begun to hang over the spotted owl. Interactions of both species make it clear that they have no inclination

Left: A young spotted owl outside its nesting cavity. Right: A spotted owl fledgling on a hemlock branch.

to crossbreed, so at least the spotties are not in danger of absorption into the barred owl gene pool.

The spotties' position is much like that of a quiet, unassuming population of aborigines, which from time out of mind has gone about its ways with unambitious, unperturbed regularity and suddenly finds itself overwhelmed by a horde of aggressive and innovative invaders. However, there is one significant difference—a third group, man, has energized itself to save these "natives" from extinction.

From the 1970s onward, the spotted owl has received more attention from conservationists than any other owl in the land. The research has been outstanding; its results are less clear.

Eric Forsman, premier authority on the spotted owl, would probably agree that despite major gains, the overall impact of conservation efforts has been diluted by a confabulation of local politics, timber industry lobbying, and bureaucrats with a pro-industry bias.

Still, a lot of eyes have been opened. And not just those of bird-listers. Saving the spotty automatically entails preserving primeval groves of Douglas fir, Sitka spruce, Ponderosa pine, and redwoods, by incorporation of integrally functioning units of mature, climax forest into the public trust*. Most spotted owl nesting areas are located in scenic canyons or ravines, and these, too, must be preserved along with adjacent clear running streams.

To put it in words that even a timber baron can understand: what the spotted owl needs to thrive is nothing less than the stuff national parks are made of. A proper spotted owl breeding site is a mini Mount Rainier. Time and again, from every conceivable angle, national parks have proved to be the most valuable real estate in the nation. Can anyone seriously argue against a chain of new miniparks in the Cascades?

The spotted owl sells itself.

---

* In April 1989, the United States Fish and Wildlife Service officially declared the spotted owl to be a threatened species. Secretary of the Interior Manuel Lujan, who a month earlier had raised the possibility of taking the teeth out of the Endangered Species Act, said he would not try to overrule this important decision of the Fish and Wildlife Service, a branch of the Department of the Interior. The decision could result in the prohibition of logging on some 1.5 million acres of virgin forest in the Pacific Northwest. The decision has been vigorously challenged by the forestry industry and powerful state and federal political factions and does not ensure a firm legal base for protecting either the forests or the owl. But it is a step in the right direction.

A spotted owl perches in a hemlock tree, waiting for prey.

GREAT GRAY OWL
(*Strix nebulosa*)

Left: An adult great gray owl perches on a branch of Douglas fir. Right: Typical habitat of the great gray owl— dense pine or fir forest.

DESCRIPTION Size 24–33 inches; wingspan 54–60 inches; tail 11–14 inches. An imposing, ash-gray owl with a huge head, long tail, big wings, and outsized facial disks framing 4–6 dark concentric rings. Yellow eyes, small for an owl, look lost in frame of rings and whitish crescent-shaped "eyebrows." Dark chin spot divides two conspicuous glossy white crescents (like bow tie or upcurved sideburns) on either side of face; these often blend with eyebrows to create striking white hourglass on dark face. Blurry pattern on breast, neck, and sides of head produces nebulous effect; older birds show much brown in plumage. Females distinctly larger than males. Often abroad by day, fearless, easily approached but can be dangerous near nest.

VOICE Main song a muffled booming: lazy series of 6–12 evenly spaced, very deep pulsing hoots— *WHVOOP-WHVOOP-WHVOOP-WHVOOP-WHVOO-WHO-HOO-HU*—like the opening beats of ruffed grouse drum roll, magnified; next-to-last note briefer, sometimes slightly stressed, last note clipped, audible only at close range. Other calls are a soft, mellow *WHOOP!* (female at nest calling to male); a *shreeek!* or *sherrick!* (food and precopulatory call, females, young); a startling outburst of heronlike squawks, squeals, wails, and barks during injury-feigning and other distraction displays.

SIMILAR SPECIES Barred and spotted owls smaller, typically darker, short-tailed, dark-eyed, lack white bow tie. Pale barred owls could be mistaken for great grays if eye color, face pattern not clearly seen.

RANGE Circumpolar. In North America nests in central Alaska and throughout most of central Canada east to south-central Ontario, south to central California (in mountains), northern Idaho, western Wyoming and Montana, northwestern Minnesota. Recent evidence of range extension into Wisconsin and Quebec. In sporadic winter flights invades prairie states, Great Lakes region, Nova Scotia, New England; has occurred as far south as Omaha, Nebraska, and Huntington, Long Island.

HABITAT Taiga forest, both evergreen and deciduous; favors tamarack bogs, islands of aspen and black poplar in spruce-pine forest; alpine meadows, subalpine forest. Winter visitors frequent brushy clearings or fields with nearby woodland border; use fenceposts, bushes, forest edge as look-outs.

NESTING   In tamarack bogs, poplar clusters, other clearings in evergreen forest; uses old nests of crows, ravens, hawks; tree stumps; ground (rarely). Tends to form loose colonies in favored areas; accepts manmade platforms. Eggs 1–9, typically 2–4, early March to July, mostly April to May. Incubation 30 days by female alone; male feeds both female and nestlings. Latter leave nest in 20–28 days, stay near nest site for up to 8 weeks.

MIGRATION   Sedentary, but turns nomadic during sporadic die-outs of voles in northern forest. In flight years scores of owls invade northern tier of states, turn up in towns and cities, often in odd places.

PREY   Small mammals, chiefly *Microtus* voles, various kinds of shrews and mice; also moles, gophers, weasels. Less frequently squirrels and rats, grouse, ducks, songbirds.

NATURAL HISTORY

Jupiter of birds, the great gray owl possesses an Olympian detachment that is one of the wonders of nature. Anecdotes about its antics abound. In Gill, Massachusetts, a tiny town on the New Hampshire border, a huge female great gray appeared one day and quickly became a local celebrity. Over 3,000 birders converged on the town to gaze at the creature filling the coffers of nearby hostelries. The Gill firemen got into the act by catching mice, which the owl obligingly gulped down after perching on the arm of the firefighter whose proud turn it was to feed this unprecedented source of municipal revenue.

When another stray appeared in Long Island, New York, it awoke one day to find a hundred people staring at it, half of them with cameras at the ready. Quickly, the owl raised a wing and held it forward. Every shutterbug understood that the bird was calling for time. Then it went into a frenzy of grooming: each leg was lifted and scrubbed; each feather of breast, back, tail, and wings was oiled and smoothed; nape, head, and face were done to a tee with the feet. Finally, the owl gave its whole frame a long, vigorous shake, allowing every feather to fall back into place, then struck a regal pose that clearly said: "Okay, fellas, start shooting; I'm ready now!"

Not only in towns but also in the wild, great grays relate to people. Loggers are often amused to see these feathered balloons float silently out of the woods, perch at point-blank range, and stare at them as they work.

Left: A great gray owlet. Above: A great gray owl atop the broken trunk of a Douglas fir, which is serving as a nesting platform.

Even intimate contacts do not seem to faze them. Dr. Robert Nero, leading Canadian authority on the species, repeatedly placed his head at the disposal of great gray owls. Many of the birds had been recently captured and might have been expected to be terrified or angry; yet, instead of raking his scalp, the owls tilted their heads, coyly closed their long-lashed eyelids, and groomed their captor's locks as solicitously as if they were the feathers of a favorite fledgling.

Great grays are not always so benign. He-imo Mikkola, owl expert nonpareil, puts it succinctly: "The aggressiveness of Great Grey Owls at the nest is probably the best known feature of their behavior." He points out that it is generally safe to approach a nest when the mother owl is sitting on eggs, but by the time the owlets are beginning to move about (i.e., when they are about ready to fledge), one should not do so without wearing a protective mask. Mikkola cites two instances of men who lost an eye and one of a man who broke a leg after being knocked off a tree, all because they visited a great gray owl nest at the wrong time.

Many other birds of prey are noted for vigorous nest defense, none perhaps surpassing the northern goshawk in this respect. A powerful steel-blue bird with red eyes and agile flight, the goshawk is the most dashing hunter of the north woods—a lynx with wings. One would think that no other bird—and certainly not the apparently placid great gray owl—would dare to stand in its way. Yet the goshawk now and then has been bested in a fair fight by the "phantom of the northern forest," as Dr. Nero has dubbed the great gray.

Goshawks do kill these owls on occasion. They are one of several limiting factors on great gray owl populations. The most potent rein, however, is the great horned owl. Indeed, as has been noted, hornies lord it over almost everything that moves above the ground, and they bully great gray owls with impunity.

The great horned owl is much heavier than the great gray (so for that matter is the snowy owl). And though the great gray does outweigh its close relative, the barred owl, it is in fact to feathers—layer upon layer of overlapping feathers—that it owes the massive look that so impresses the observer.

This has led authors questing for cute phrases to twit the great gray owl repeatedly, creating a cumulative effect in the literature that is totally misleading. One statement, repeated to exhaustion, was made by a Rhode Island taxidermist who once mounted one: "Taken all in all, it is the most bird for the least

Top: A great gray owl lights upon its nesting platform. Above: A great gray owlet swallows a vole head first.

body, rare to the point of alarm and yet showing occasional signs of abundance, it has in recent years received much attention from investigators on both sides of the Atlantic, notably Nero in North America and Mikkola in the Old World.

And the more it is studied, the more puzzles arise. None is as intriguing as the one posed by the behavior Nero calls "snow plung-

substance we ever examined." Clearly, neither he nor any of the scores of scientists who have quoted him ever lost an eye or nursed a broken leg after being attacked by an impetuous great gray owl.

A full-grown female great gray owl may tip the scales at four pounds; its head will be over twenty inches in circumference. There are reliable reports of individuals with wingspreads of close to six feet.

An owl of such dimensions, known to be able to hold its own against a goshawk and demonstrably able to maim human beings, is hardly a creature of little substance.

The great gray owl is, indeed, a bird of paradox. Majestic yet quaint, huge of head and long of plume but relatively sparse of

A great gray owl presents its prey, a vole, to two owlets at the nest.

ing." In deep snow mice and voles tunnel up to the surface to breathe. It is at the holes through which they poke their little whiskered snouts that owls typically grab them. Many great grays, however, just don't seem to want to wait for them to come up for air. Instead they dive, headfirst, into the snow and fish them out!

How, from a height of thirty feet, do the owls sense the presence of a mouse under a foot or more of dense snow? (They almost never come up empty-handed.) How do they manage never to break their necks on a hard buried object—log or rock? No one knows. And probably no one ever will.

That's what makes the great gray owl so fascinating. Just when you think you understand it, the bird hands you another surprise.

LONG-EARED OWL
(*Asio otus*)

Left: An adult long-eared owl perches in a fir tree. Right: Typical long-eared owl habitat—dense forest cover, mixed hardwoods, and evergreens or conifers.

DESCRIPTION

Size 13–16 inches; wingspan 36–42 inches. A slim medium-size owl with prominent ear tufts set close together, brilliant orange eyes. Facial disks rich burnt orange in east, light tawny in pale western race. Eastern birds show blend of brown and tawny; in western birds mix of dusky and white gives grayish cast. Boldly patterned below with crosshatched lengthwise streaks. Long dark wings have inconspicuous buff patch at base of primaries, small black crescent below at "wrist." Strictly nocturnal. Most often seen in winter roosts in conifer groves, thickets. Flight buoyant, mothlike.

VOICE

Repertoire near nest rivals that of barred owl. Not as vocal elsewhere, but far less silent than references indicate. Most often heard: a soft single or double hoot—*quoo* or *quoo-quoo*—remarkably pure and musical, given in long, leisurely series by both sexes; a long, quavering *WHOOooo*, with haunted house quality; rhythmic groups of three snappy barks—*wreck-wreck-wreck!*—uttered by both sexes, sometimes in flight, like pair of puppies yelping forty feet above ground (changes to gull-like *wak-wak-wak* in west); catlike whines and wails, often with snarly ending. During distraction display utters startling medley of squeals, whines, mews, and shrieks.

SIMILAR SPECIES

Great horned owl bigger, stouter, barred crosswise beneath. Screech owls smaller, chunky. In flight difficult to distinguish from short-eared owl: long-eareds are darker, stockier, lack pale band on trailing edge of wing; wrist mark and buff patch on under and upper wing less prominent than on short-eared owl.

RANGE

In broad temperate belt across North America, Eurasia, and parts of Africa. In North America breeds from southern Mackenzie and central British Columbia east across central Canada to Quebec and Nova Scotia; south to northwest Baja California and east across Arizona, New Mexico, west Texas, Oklahoma, and Arkansas to Virginia. Winters south to Mexico, Gulf states, Florida, and Bermuda. Vagrant to Alaska, Cuba.

HABITAT In northern part of range favors edges of dense or semiopen evergreen or mixed evergreen-broadleaf forest; tree belts along prairie streams; thickly wooded canyons, pinyon-juniper scrubland; desert oases; riparian groves. Less frequently farm woodlots, timbered parkland.

NESTING In abandoned nests of magpies, herons, hawks, or crows (has been known to evict crows from active nest); also squirrel dreys; cavities in trees; ground (rare). Can build own nest but rarely does. Eggs 3–8, typically 4–5, from March to July, typically April. Incubation, by female, 21–28 days; owlets leave nest 23–26 days after hatching, fly when 5 weeks old.

MIGRATION Partial migrant. Birds in northern part of range move south in winter; variable but regular fall migrant in northeast, probably elsewhere; notable October-November coastal flights in migration cul-de-sacs such as Cape May, New Jersey. Noted for displacement movements from inland localities to winter roosts along coasts.

PREY Predominantly small mammals, chiefly *Microtus* voles, mice, shrews. Birds comprise less than 2 percent of diet; rarely small snakes, frogs, beetles. Known to have killed screech and saw-whet owls.

Right: A long-eared owl hatchling not more than two weeks old. Far right: A subadult long-eared owl.

NATURAL HISTORY

The long-eared is the archetypal owl. No other owl has a hoot so pure, plumage so cryptic, or eyes so hypnotic. As a mouser it rivals the barn owl. And no other owl has more mysterious ways.

More gaps remain in our knowledge of the natural history of the long-eared owl than in that of any other species of similar range. Long-eareds nest chiefly in fairly accessible areas of the north temperate belt. In winter they gather in often impressive roosts—up to fifty owls have been seen in a single evergreen grove. As owls go, they are relatively easy to identify. Why then are they considered an enigma?

First of all because no one seems to be able to find them during the nesting season. No one, that is, except—and it is a very significant exception—owlers in certain areas of the West, where the birds nest in islands of suitable hab-

The Owls of North America: Long-Eared Owl 109

itat, surrounded by "seas" where they would be, so to speak, fish out of water. In the second place, the winter roosts give clear evidence of their abundance, yet we don't know where they come from.

It is important for the reader to realize that long-eared owls with nestlings are not shy about proclaiming the fact. In contrast with great gray and great horned owls, they seldom dive-bomb an intruder. However, in one's presence, they will drop to the ground, roll about, shriek, whine, and all told put up a ruckus that resembles a performance by a punk-rock band.

Despite all this, every time a family of long-eareds is found there is jubilation in the field glass fraternity. Why should these owls be so hard to find?

One possible explanation is that their homesteads are widely scattered: the ample woodlands of Pennsylvania, New York, and northern New England, not to mention the vast timberlands of Canada, may harbor an impressive number of long-eared nests and yet allow for huge expanses of intervening habitat completely untenanted by the birds. This writer, however, proposes what he believes to be a more cogent theory. Long-eared owls are masters of concealment. One of their best-known tricks is freezing against a tree trunk, making themselves look exactly like a stick or a broken stub. But the owls place too much confidence in the effectiveness of this camouflage. Though it baffles human birders, it clearly does not deceive those sharp-eyed bird finders, other birds of prey. Goshawks and horned owls have no trouble spotting a long-eared and making a meal out of it. And the bird's habit of defending its nest with an excess of visual and vocal histrionics does not help to make it a less accessible target.

Whatever the case, long-eared owls only too often wind up in the pellets of other owls. No other species is so frequently killed and eaten by others of its tribe. In Eurasia its chief enemy is the eagle owl. The great horned owl, the eagle owl's New World counterpart, is the chief nemesis of the long-eared owl in North America, where it is also subject to predation by barred and spotted owls.

There can be little doubt that this predator pressure is the key factor accounting for the oddly disjointed distribution of long-eareds.

An adult long-eared owl and four juveniles at nest in a ponderosa pine.

Certainly, the absence of larger, more aggressive hawks and owls in the state forest at Martha's Vineyard has played a major role in helping the long-eared owl gain a foothold in this large artificial rectangle of cultivated evergreens. In this popular birding spot the owl in fact appears to be the dominant predator.

The Niche Switch

In most respects, except numbers, the long-eared owl is the nocturnal counterpart of the broad-winged hawk. The broad-wing, an abundant mid-September migrant, is the star of fall flights at raptor watcher meccas like Hawk Mountain, Pennsylvania. A mid-size *Buteo*, it is intermediate in both shape and habits between the red-tailed and red-shouldered hawks. In turn, the long-eared is intermediate between the great horned owl,

nocturnal equivalent of the red-tailed hawk, and the barred, which replaces the red-shoulder after sundown.

Long-eareds and broad-wings have a similar range and similar habitat preferences. Whereas horned owls and red-tails choose clearings close to hilly woodlands and barred owls and red-shoulders prefer lowland swamps, the broad-wings and long-eareds stick to a happy medium in the heart of the woods. The first life style they would deem too dry, the second too wet; their own, they might claim, is just right, the raptorial golden mean.

This triad of ecological niche switches admirably sums up the economy of nature—except for one biotope, the open marsh. That is the bailiwick of the short-eared owl, close congener of the long-eared and subject of our next portrait.

SHORT-EARED OWL
(*Asio flammeus*)

Left: An adult short-eared owl perches on a fencepost. Right: Typical short-eared owl habitat—deep grass fields and woodlands.

DESCRIPTION

Size 13–17 inches; wingspan 38–44 inches. A buff-colored diurnal owl of dunes, marshes, prairies, tundra. Ear tufts small, seldom seen. Lemon-yellow eyes set off in cusps of blackish feathers, framed between white eyebrow-whisker hourglass and pale outer feathers of face. Tawny above, mottled and striped with darker brown; pale buff below, with dark streaks on neck and upper breast, fading on belly. Some birds grayish. In flight, wing shows buff patch above, black crescent below "wrist," pale band along trailing edge, black tips. Nicknamed "loper" for distinctive buoyant, shifting flight, like huge tipsy moth; looks big-headed, "neckless." Gregarious away from nest; gathers in often large winter roosts.

VOICE

Love song "a low-pitched, hollow *boo-boo-boo-boo,* resembling the distant, slow puffing of an old steam engine" (Mikkola); 16–20 *boos* delivered from perch or during display flight; female answers with raspy snarl—*whreee-yéeeough!* Many variants of snarl used by both sexes in and out of nesting season. Often heard: a harsh *keeé-erp!,* a shrill, penetrating squeal—*shreEEEehrp!*—like knife being sharpened on motor-driven whetstone; emphatic high-pitched yelps in pairs or triplets—*wrick-wrick!* or *wrick-wrick-wrick!*—like yapping terrier, in solo series or as preface to snarl—*wrick-wrick-skree-yéeeow!* At nest, medley of squeals, hoarse barks, raucous nasal meows. Like most owls, hisses loudly, snaps bill.

SIMILAR SPECIES

See long-eared owl. Barn owl paler, unstreaked, dark-eyed, has snow-white heart-shaped face. Two hawks with similar markings share habits and habitat: northern harrier slimmer, small-headed, has white rump; rough-legged hawk (light phase) has broad black band on belly, white tail with wide black band at end, much different profile, heavier flight. American bittern, immature night heron, seen in flight from behind, can be confusing in bad light.

RANGE

Many oceanic islands, all continents except Australia. In North America from western Alaska east across arctic Canada to Newfoundland, south locally in suitable habitat to central California, east across north-central states to New Jersey. Rapidly vanishing from many nesting areas. Winters in Mexico, Gulf states, Florida.

HABITAT Marshes, moors, dunes, grasslands, tundra, other open country. Patrols ground at dawn and dusk, perches on clumps, hides in hummocks, lies with belly on sand; also perches on fence-posts, muskrat houses, duck blinds; roosts in hedgerows, border brushland, conifers near marsh.

NESTING On ground, sometimes in loose colonies, often close to northern harrier. Often builds own nest (one of few owls to do so), a shallow scrape thinly lined with grass, feathers, stubble, in open or in shelter of bush, heather clump, fallen tree; may just use flattened vegetation. Rarely old tree nest, excavated burrow, ledge, stump. Eggs 2–14 (extremes), usually 4–7, March to mid-June. Female incubates 3–4 weeks; owlets fly 25–35 days after hatching. Parents known to move eggs and young to escape tides, protect nestlings with "crippled bird" diversion.

MIGRATION Known for tremendous nomadic flights, sometimes over ocean; has uncanny ability to sense rodent population explosions, turns up in hundreds in plague areas. Winters in nesting area if rodent food available, but each year many birds fly south to regions noted above.

PREY Main food is meadow mice (*Microtus*); takes many other rodents, shrews, rabbits, bats; many kinds of insects. If pressed becomes bird hunter, taking meadowlarks, "grass" sparrows, et cetera, woodland species at migration cul-de-sacs; known to have preyed on nesting terns and, remarkably, rails (sora, black).

NATURAL HISTORY

The Mercury of owls, this fleet day-flying hunter can outdistance a jackrabbit fleeing at full tilt. Thus nature has insured the short-eared owl against lean times with the equipment it needs to chase a rabbit or a bird when its favorite food, the plump and usually prolific vole, happens to run out. Such scarcity of food occurs every three or four years in different parts of the bird's vast range.

Considering that twelve kinds of owls consume voles by the barrel and that five species would eat nothing else if given the chance, a few words about these animals are in order. Voles, also called meadow mice (in scientific parlance, the various species in the genus *Microtus*), are stocky, short-tailed rodents with well-fleshed hindquarters. Resembling a cross between a mouse and a mole, and often unbelievably abundant, they are subject along with many other small rodents to periodic boom-bust cycles. Boom, of course, begets boom; mice proliferate and so do the predators that feast on them. But fast will always follow feast, and in the ensuing crash the now overabundant hunters must wander in search of quarry or perish.

Fortunately, voles do not plummet simultaneously over huge areas, as does, for example, the snowshoe hare. There is always some spot where these fat-fannied kernel chompers are on the upswing. This gives the short-eared owl a chance to put on one of the most spectacular acts in the bird world.

In some locality voles will suddenly erupt and overrun the place. Almost overnight a horde of short-eared owls, unsuspected in the vicinity, will materialize seemingly out of nowhere, descend upon the varmints, gobble them up, and move on . . . where to one can only guess.

This ability is shared by other birds. The California gull—the species the Mormons of Salt Lake City memorialized in marble for saving their crops from a cricket plague—has it. Still, when owls perform the trick they reach heights of drama unknown to any gull. A few years ago voles swarmed over Amherst Island on Lake Ontario. Short-eareds by the dozen poured in out of the void; more amazingly, they brought along a retinue: great gray owls, snowy owls, hawk owls, boreal owls, and saw-whet owls in unprecedented numbers festooned the island. The writer recalls the late great ornithologist, Bob Arbib, describing a tree in which half a dozen short-eared owls, two snowies, three great grays, four boreals, and a handful of saw-whet owls sat together, groggily digesting a surfeit of the polyprogenitive and delectable meadow mice.

As shy, retiring, and difficult to find as the long-eared owl usually is, the short-eared owl is bold, outgoing, and as owls go, fairly easy to add to one's life list. Just as the winsome burrowing owl often gives nature lovers their first glimpse of owldom in billy country, this improbably beautiful extrovert has created more than one strixine addict in its many purlieus across the land.

Short-eared owls are versatile. In pursuit of a jackrabbit through the sagebrush the floppy wingbeats of a hunting short-eared will change instantly to a power stroke reminiscent of a gyrfalcon in a strafing attack. If, when quartering over a meadow, the owl thinks it might be a good idea to investigate a promising gopher burrow, it will stop suddenly in midair and hover like a kestrel; if the hoped-for meal materializes the owl will quickly drop down and snatch the gopher in a classic example of pounce technique. It also, of course, picks up prey in glides and swoops. When a wave of northbound songbirds crosses Lake Ontario in a fog-bound April night and crashes on a sand spit on the Canadian shore, the owl is prepared for the occasion: having chosen to perch on a driftwood stump, of which it looks like an extension, our bird is waiting to breakfast on vireos and warblers, as confident in its camouflage as a whippoorwill on a bed of oak leaves.

Short-eared owls are courageous, energetic, and playful. They dislike being mobbed—it is really most undignified—and instead of taking it on the nose (as even great horned owls usually do) they will turn tables on their assailants and send them flying for their lives. Crows, being frequent mobbers, are frequent victims.

Once in a while a great blue heron comes in for a shock. These huge, stately waders, with their long, rapierlike bills and their six-foot wingspreads, think they own the marsh and often assert themselves by skewering creatures not ordinarily considered heron fare, like the young of other marsh birds. The owls know this and are only too delighted when a heron wings its way, majestic but ponderous, within striking range. At this moment the loper's aerobatic capabilities are put to devastating use, owl outmaneuvering heron with ease, delivering telling blows at the big bird's hackles, dive-bombing it from above, slamming it on the sides, and all told, turning his majesty of the marsh into a pitiable fugitive, flopping for dear life and emitting doleful croaks.

The short-eared owl can and will, improbable as it may seem, outfly the northern harrier (or marsh hawk, as it used to be called), one of the most agile of hawks and a bird with which the short-eared lives mostly on friendly terms, as will shortly be seen. However, once in a while, a short-eared will engage a harrier in a dogfight. This—one of the grandest sights a bird watcher can hope to see—can be observed in places as distant and different as Netarts Bay, Oregon, and Brigantine National Wildlife Refuge, near Atlantic City, New Jersey. The encounter, usually just a contest of aviatorial skill almost always ending in a draw, is, nevertheless, one of the most thrilling exhibitions of flying virtuosity that nature has to offer.

Short-eared owls are raffish. Courting males will begin their aerial display by flying with exceptionally slow wingbeats, each stroke accompanied by a snappy upward jerk. They will keep on gaining altitude until they are barely a speck in the blue. Then the bird will begin a series of short, slanting dives, each ending with an upward swoop, like a small buff-colored blimp running on the tracks of an improbably high, invisible roller coaster. When the owl starts each dive it brings its long wings together beneath its body, stretches them backward, and rapidly claps them together, producing a sound much like the fluttering of a flag in gale. The rate of wing clapping is remarkably fast, from four to eight beats per second. Between bouts of diving and wing clapping, the lusty suitor will add to the efficacy of his wooing by intoning a serenade, filling the air with the puffing *boo-boo-boos* so quaintly compared by Heimo Mikkola to the coughing of a decrepit steam engine. The entire performance, though usually crepuscular, is often given in broad daylight.

The Niche Switch

The courtship of the short-eared, in addition to being elaborate and dramatic for an owl, vividly underscores the remarkable degree of convergence that this species exhibits vis-à-vis the northern harrier, its replacement species among the diurnal raptors. There is no more perfect example of the niche-switch phenomenon that so beautifully illuminates the dynamics of ecosystem utilization.

An adult short-eared owl presents a mouse to its young in the nest.

Courting harriers go through feats of aerobatic foreplay almost identical to those of the short-eared owl. A roller-coastering male harrier, were it not for the bright white rump, could easily be mistaken at a distance for this bird.

How evolutionary convergence has closed the gap between hawk and owl is well illustrated by similarity of anatomical detail. Harriers are the most owllike of hawks; they have prominent facial disks, which they use to great advantage in detecting voles by sound while hugging the contours of the land, tilting their heads from side to side, ears cocked to pick up any telltale rustle in the reeds. Short-eareds hunt in much the same manner.

Owl and hawk nest close to each other and seldom get into backyard squabbles. In winter, they even roost together, often in considerable aggregations, irresistibly recalling a coterie of old cronies playing pinochle in the park and trading time-worn yarns.

BOREAL OWL
(*Aegolius funereus*)

Left: An adult boreal owl returns to its nest, where an owlet awaits food, in this case a mouse. Right: Typical boreal owl habitat—the boreal conifer belt.

DESCRIPTION Size 8–12 inches; wingspan 19–25 inches. A small owl of the boreal forest, with a big flat-topped head and a striking face pattern: high arches on white facial disks, dark widow's peak densely stippled with white give it a look of constant surprise. Black rim of facial disk converges on dark ringlets around golden-yellow eyes. Bill usually horn-colored or yellowish. Upper parts chocolate brown with bold white spots; white below with soft tawny streaks; birds range from russet to grayish. Juveniles uniform sooty brown with blackish faces, shallow white V on forehead. Females notably larger and heavier than males. Nocturnal. Extremely confiding but easy to overlook.

VOICE Spring song, one of finest owl voices, a series of 5–10 rich whistled notes—*hoo-poo-poo-poo-poo*—in groups of 5–6 pulsing *poos* with 1–2 second pauses between groups, like call of Eurasian hoopoe, or in rapid run, rising at end, like winnowing snipe. (References to call as like sound of dripping water probably due to confusion with saw-whet owl; comparison to tolling bell based on famous but flawed account.) Contact calls include a hollow *hooh;* alarm call a sharp down-slurred *chéeaw!;* various other shrill calls. Usually silent in winter.

SIMILAR SPECIES Saw-whet owl smaller, crown and forehead finely streaked, not spotted, bill black, facial disk buff, lacks black rim, stripes below ochre rust; juveniles cinnamon-buff below, with dark brown faces. Hawk owl (similar face pattern) larger, long-tailed, boldly barred below. Screech owls often flatten ear tufts; boreals sometimes raise forehead feathers, creating short horns; look for boreal face pattern (screech owls lack white on face).

RANGE Boreal forests of northern hemisphere. In North America from Alaska across subarctic Canada to Newfoundland, south to British Columbia (recent reports from Washington), Idaho, and Colorado (mountains), northern Minnesota (where first U.S. nest found), northern Michigan, extreme northern New York and New England, southern Quebec and New Brunswick (Grand Manan). Winters in and just south of breeding range. In irruptive flights south to Oregon, Nebraska, New Jersey.

HABITAT	Conifers, chiefly spruce, but also mixed woodlands of pine, poplar, birch; subalpine evergreens, pine forests on lower slopes. Winter wanderers found in igloos, barns, haystacks, other odd places.
NESTING	Holes in trees; prefers old nests of pileated woodpeckers but uses other woodpecker holes, natural cavities; accepts nesting box. Eggs 3–10, usually 4–6, from March to June, usually April to May. Incubation, by female, 25–30 days; fledging 28–32 days.
MIGRATION	Usually described as resident species, but periodically migrates in response to 3–4 year fluctuations in breeding rate of boreal rodents. Strong evidence supports theory that adult males are sedentary, females and young nomadic.
PREY	Small mammals (over 90 percent), mostly woodland voles (*Clethrionomys*); also lemmings, meadow mice (*Microtus*), white-footed mice, shrews; small birds (5 percent). Insect consumption negligible, contra published reports.

A boreal owl perches on a spruce branch in a northern forest. The boreal owl is strictly nocturnal and uses dense evergreens to hide from marauding ravens, crows, and jays.

NATURAL HISTORY

The winsome little boreal owl has several distinctions: it is on the most wanted list of every birder who hasn't seen one; it is one of the most highly evolved of all owls; it has been given more names* than even so advanced an owl has a right to—a source of mild confusion; and its call was misidentified early in the century by no less a giant than Ernest Thompson Seton—a source of colossal confusion.

The last "distinction" is one of the more curious episodes in the often fitful evolution of our knowledge of the natural world. The redoubtable Seton rarely made mistakes, and in regard to the calls of the boreal owl he did not in fact make one. What he did was trust the word of another naturalist, Edward Preble, a recognized expert on the arctic fauna. Preble's knowledge of boreal owl calls was based partly on misinterpreted field experience and partly on information gathered from the work of John Richardson, after whom the New World race of *Aegolius funereus* had been baptized Richardson's owl.

Richardson simply didn't know the song of the bird that bore his name; poor Preble didn't either, and he passed the misinformation on to Seton, who handed it down to posterity in his *Arctic Prairies,* published in 1911. Since then scores of scientists have quoted the charmingly worded but misleading "Love Song of the Richardson's Owl" passage in that epoch-making book.

What happened was this. Preble and Seton were camping in Alberta on the Athabaska River, across from Fort McKay. At about ten at night Preble put his head in the tent where Seton was lying and said, "Come out here if you want a new sensation." The sensation, so Seton was persuaded, was the courtship call of the boreal owl. What it actually was is hard to say, since neither man really *saw* the bird, but Seton's description overwhelmingly suggests the spring song of either a saw-whet or a pygmy owl. In any case, it does not fit the distinctive song of the boreal owl, given above.

The boreal owl is a nocturnal forest hunter. Typically, it frequents the denser parts of the woods, such as the often impenetrable stands of spruce and fir that line the bogs and ravines of the taiga. Agile on the wing, the boreal flies nimbly around thick vegetation. It will not, however, hesitate to abandon its woodland haunts when word goes out in owlish that an explosion of meadow mice in some outlying pasture holds the promise of easy and plentiful fare. On such occasions, as well as in the high arctic, where the summer sun never sets, the bird readily takes to daylight hunting. Necessity, with owls as with people, is the mother of invention.

Nevertheless, by far the favorite living quarters of the boreal owl are located in the deep green gloom of humid evergreen forests, where scarlet berries of the dwarf dogwood glisten atop emerald carpets of moss beneath a

---

* Boreal, Richardson's, Tengmalm's (Europe), and artic saw-whet.

Left: A juvenile boreal owl perches alongside a rodent just delivered by one of its parents. Above: A young boreal owl.

dense canopy of spruces festooned with mistletoe and blue-gray webs of the usnea lichen or old-man's beard.

In this fairy tale setting the owl hunts by perching on a low limb and peering intently at the richly textured ground. It uses its extraordinarily asymmetrical ear openings (the right one is much higher than the left; see illustration on page 144) to locate with uncanny precision the source of any rustle or squeak on the forest floor. A shrew or redback vole, whether seen or heard, is approached on a silent glide. A fraction of a second before the strike, the bird will close its eyes, tilt its head backward, thrust its talons forward, and spread out its wings to act as a brake.

The technique is extraordinarily efficient. Short-eared owls, gifted hunters though they be, miss two-thirds of their strikes; the boreals reverse the ratio, scoring two times out of three. This is all the more remarkable when one considers that a lemming or redback vole is a pretty big animal, sometimes approaching the body size of a boreal. Hearing (or seeing) the beastie and striking it hardly insure success. The talons must be perfectly focused on the center of gravity of the future meal lest it manage to squirm away. Once the quarry is secured, the owl administers a few lethal blows to the head with its beak—the strixine equiv-

alent of culinary preparation—and dinner is ready. In this context it is interesting to note that hawks and falcons are more dainty; they often put in a good deal of time plucking their victims and carving out choice tidbits.

A curious habit of the boreal owl is to respond to intruders that seem to threaten their nests by completely plugging the entrance to the nest hole with their heads. Peering out at the potential enemy while adjusting the outer rim of the facial disk to fit the perimeter of the cavity seems an odd way to prevent a marten, that champion arboreal weasel, from eating a batch of baby boreal owlets. But one must remember that a carnivore will almost never try to bite its prey head-on—even lions will try to grab a gazelle from the side. The owl's sharp bill aimed at the snout of a marten will make the latter think twice before attempting to strike. A hunter cannot afford to get hurt— a wounded weasel is almost surely an ineffectual foe of lemmings and hares, let alone owls.

This method of nest defense has long been known to owl finders, who years ago mastered the trick of tapping trees with cavities likely to harbor breeding boreal owls. Indeed, treetapping is one of the time-honored strategies for finding the boreal owl's closest relative— subject of our next and final portrait—the cunning little saw-whet owl.

NORTHERN SAW-WHET OWL
(Aegolius acadicus)

Left: An adult saw-whet owl hunts by day beneath the dark canopy of an Olympic rain forest in Washington state. Right: An adult saw-whet owl is almost concealed by pussy willow branches.

DESCRIPTION Size 7–8½ inches; wingspan 17–21 inches. A very small tuftless owl of the cool, moist woods, with a remarkably gentle expression. Head looks huge in proportion to body; crown, forehead, and edges of face finely streaked with white; golden-yellow eyes look like roundish almonds framed by white face mask, large, pale buff facial disks; black bill. Upper parts reddish brown with bold white spots on wings; underparts show bright cinnamon streaks on white background. Colorful juvenile has rich mahogany brown face and upper parts, broad white V on forehead, bright cinnamon breast, buff belly. Ridiculously tame, but small, nocturnal, easily overlooked. Most often seen in winter roosts.

VOICE Spring song "a mellow whistled note repeated mechanically in endless succession, often 100–130 per minute: *too, too, too, too, too, too,* etc." (Roger Tory Peterson). Tooting, often two-syllabled, ranges from flattish to bell-like, is highly ventriloquial; a harsh *skree-aw!,* typically heard after dawn; a descending melancholy wail—*pheeuh, pheeuh, pheeuh, pheeuh*—fading at end; fall migrants repeatedly give snappy, down-slurred whistles; variety of shrill discordant calls, none frequent and none resembling sound of saw being whetted.

SIMILAR SPECIES Boreal owl has whitish, black-rimmed face disks, fine white spots on crown and forehead. Pygmy owls have long barred tails, eyespots on nape, fly by day; calls can be confused (for details see Northern Pygmy Owl, page 67). Flammulated owl has dark eyes; it and screech owls both tufted, lack white face mask. Separation from screech owls on basis of call in areas of sporadic overlap can be difficult; saw-whets typically substitute medley of wails, whinnies, and squeals for characteristic courtship song.

RANGE Breeds from southwest Alaska south through British Columbia and most of western U.S. into central Mexico; east across central Canada to Nova Scotia; south to central U.S. (except in prairies); and in East south to highlands of New Jersey, continuing in mountains to South Carolina (Mt. Mitchell). Winters throughout breeding range and south erratically to Mexican border, Arkansas, Louisiana, Tennessee, coastal Carolinas, Georgia, north Florida.

HABITAT Coniferous forest bordering wetlands with lush deciduous growth; also mixed stands, swamps, woodlots. In winter favors evergreen thickets, dense brushy tangles in estates, parks, yards; occasionally in isolated evergreen. Some birds use same site repeatedly during season, occasionally in consecutive years.

NESTING Typically cavities in dead stubs, mostly old nests of northern flicker, less often pileated or other woodpeckers; accepts properly placed birdhouse (has nested in wood duck boxes); natural nest sites typically swampy or close to water. Eggs 4–7, usually 5–6, March to July, usually April to May. Incubation, almost exclusively by female, 25–30 days; young fly 4 to 5 weeks after hatching.

MIGRATION Numbers fluctuate, but regular October-November flights along shores of western Great Lakes region often remarkable; flies south in same season along Atlantic seaboard. Northbound migrants reach New England and Great Lakes in March. Migration less well documented in West. Irruptive flights follow periods of prey scarcity in northern woods.

PREY Woodland rodents such as mice, chipmunks, and baby squirrels; young rats, shrews, and bats; occasionally songbirds such as warblers, juncos, sparrows; known to hunt insects on ground and on wing.

NATURAL HISTORY

The saw-whet owl, or Acadian Adorable, as Jonathan Maslow calls it, is an irresistibly engaging animal. Even the coldest scientists have been known to melt at the sight of this doe-eyed darling. Katy Duffy, head of the owl banding program at Cape May, New Jersey, says no one can overcome the temptation to pet a saw-whet owl. In fact the bird has been called cute, cuddly, quaint, charming, winsome, and endearing so often that one is tempted to counter that it is really a nasty, vicious, and cruel creature.

The argument would fail miserably. What can you say against an owl that flies into your tent, perches for a bit, sings you a song or two, and then flies out to rejoin its comrades in a moonlit mouse hunt? That struts up to the kitchen of a suburban estate, tries to groom the dog, sniffs the begonias, then ambles off into the woods? Or that gets caught in a mist net on a rainy Saturday, is brought by the bird bander into his motel room, eats hamburger out of his hand, perches on a lamp shade, and watches a football game on TV? The stories are legion.

A close relative of the boreal owl, the saw-whet differs from the former both in its range and in its greater consumption of insects. Two factors underlie the dietary difference. One is that where saw-whets live there is a wider variety of insects. The other is that they are adept at rapid, shifting flight: many observers have noted how closely the flight of the saw-whet resembles that of a woodcock. This agility enables the saw-whet to catch insects in the air. Significantly, screech owls do the same thing. Saw-whets, moreover, are exceptional mousers; in certain areas they are likely to go after the beasties in fields adjacent to wooded wetlands—again, much like screech owls.

Far left: A saw-whet owl with a vole in its beak, to be delivered to hungry young in the nesting cavity. Left: A saw-whet owlet peers from its nest cavity. Below: An adult owl prepares to leave the nest after feeding its young.

A catcher of mice and moths that nests in flicker holes decidedly encroaches on the ecological niche of the screech owl. Saw-whets and screechers do not get along, and the foregoing makes it easy to see why this should be so. What may not be obvious is what this implies in terms of the range of the saw-whet. To some degree the breeding distribution of this species is determined by the availability of proper habitat. But the normal southern limit of its breeding range, and in all probability its altitudinal limits in western mountains and in the southern Appalachians, are set by a key limiting factor—competition from the stronger, more aggressive screech owl.

In the springs that follow unusually heavy fall and winter flights, many saw-whet owls do not fly back to their homesteads in the cool, moist conifers of the north. Instead they find and try to colonize attractive chunks of southern real estate that by rights are the bailiwick of the screech owl. The intruding saw-whets usually succeed in gaining a precarious toehold on the territory and brag about it in night after night of incessant tooting. It is thus easy to be misled into believing that they have brought about a southward extension of their range. The newcomers may hold their own for one or two nesting seasons, but eventually the screech owls rally, reassert their claim, and restore the original balance of owlish power.

One of the most fascinating and well-documented facets of the life of saw-whet owls is their remarkable migrations. In Duluth, Minnesota, David Evans has thoroughly documented the sometimes spectacular flights that take place in October along the shores of Lake Superior. In Cape May similar movements have been monitored by Katy Duffy. If the number of owls caught in her nets is not as impressive as the totals tallied by Evans it may well be because the southern terminus of migration for Atlantic Flyway birds is often a thicket or copse in southern New Jersey or adjacent Pennsylvania, Delaware, and Maryland. Saw-whets, in fact, have long been known to congregate in large winter roosts along the shores of Delaware Bay; however, most of the wooded areas that harbored these roosts have vanished in the wake of industrial development. As of this writing intense efforts are being made to preserve some of the tracts that from time out of mind have been the winter haven of these exquisite little nomads. It is to be hoped that nature lovers years from now will be able to enjoy the beauty that preserving such habitats will provide, including a glimpse of the loveliest of our owls.

Saw-whet fledglings perch in a pine tree.

How the Saw-Whet Got Its Name

Even more confusing than what has been written about the calls of the boreal owl is the tangle of contradictions woven on the subject of how the saw-whet got its name. Yards of rhetoric have been expended in attempts to persuade readers (and the authors themselves, one suspects by their tortured arguments) that one of the common calls of this species resembles the sound of a lumber mill saw being filed. The birds do give vent to a variety of shrill and discordant sounds. None, however, matches the sound of a file being drawn repeatedly across the teeth of a mill saw, and none, in any case, is uttered frequently enough for a folk name to have been derived from it.

This leaves the often cited *skree-aw!* call to be accounted for. In none of the many references to this sound, including eloquent passages in Angus Cameron's *Nightwatchers* and William Brewster's classic monograph on the birds of Lake Umbagog, is evidence presented that this call is anything but a subordinate vocalization, or one that farmers and trappers of yesteryear might have traced back to an owl that is almost impossible to see when it sings at night in the heart of a spruce tree!

What saw-whets typically do is toot. The sound is sometimes bell-like, sometimes flat. It changes volume as the male aims its love notes around by rotating its head. The toots are often doubled. Very excited birds may utter a quick succession of nervous two-syllabled whistles. The rhythm, therefore, is variable, as is the tonal quality. Even the structure of the utterance itself may change. The constantly repeated snappy squeals of fall migrants can be shrill. Two things are common in all normal instances of saw-whet song: monotony and just about total lack of resemblance to saws being whetted.

Fortunately, a more plausible explanation lies ready at hand. As Davis Finch pointed out years ago, the name of the owl is almost certainly an anglicization of the French word *chouette* (shoo-ET), a word universally used in France and French Canada to refer to any small owl. *La chouette* is indeed what farmers in the Gaspé and elsewhere in French-speaking Canada call this little owl, which for them is a backyard species.

The anglicized version of the word probably arose out of interactions between American north country woodsmen and their Québecois counterparts. One need only imagine an Acadian campsite at which a moose and bear tracker from Calais, Maine, hears a beaver hunter from Rivière du Loup say, "Ça? Ça

c'est la chouette!" in answer to the Yankee's request for the name of an absurdly confiding little owl he has just caught napping in the bough of a spruce sapling. When one further takes into account that many French Canadians substitute an *s* sound for the initial *ch* and say *soo-WET,* the derivation becomes even more likely.

With such a simple explanation available, why has the saw-filing etymology hung on so long? Because it has a lofty provenance. It was concocted by no less than the great John James Audubon. In 1811 Audubon settled in Henderson, Kentucky, eventually doing well enough to buy a mill. But the mill turned out to be a white elephant in more ways than one. Not only did it ruin Audubon financially, it also led to some rather preposterous ornithology.

One hot summer day Audubon heard shrill sounds coming from inside the mill. Attributing these to an owl (albeit one he never saw clearly), he thought he detected a similarity between the song and the back-and-forth scrapings of a whetstone or file on a large lumber saw. Then he remembered that folks up in New England spoke of a bird they called the saw-whet owl. Promptly, he decided that his bird was one of these. And he decided as well that the reason folks up north called *their* birds by that funny name was that they made the same noise as his midsummer Kentucky day-calling, mill-roosting, raspy-voiced owl!

Never mind that saw-whets are likely to visit Henderson only in the dead of winter; never mind that they call neither during the day nor in midsummer and will roost inside a grist mill only if they are tied up in it; never mind that Audubon's foreman—who *had* seen the owl clearly—told him it was a "Screech Owl," a universal term for the barn owl among local farm folk of that era.

What Audubon heard, then, were the cries of a nesting barn owl. That's a call that really sounds like a saw being whetted! But these were the Henderson days, when the great John James had not found his footing and was playing cruel jokes on Constantin Rafinesque by inventing nonexistent birds and fishes. So why not a fanciful story about an owl?

The story, later polished up and inserted in Audubon's *Ornithological Biographies,* has served posterity oddly by providing a colorful but deceptive solution to the puzzle of the bird's name.

A pair of saw-whet owls on a winter hunt in a lowland western forest.

7

ANATOMY

Left: *A juvenile long-eared owl in flight.* Right: *Detail of snowy owl feathers.*

BONES, MUSCLES, AND TENDONS

*A*n owl on the wing is not fast— short-eared and hawk owls are the exception—but it is nonetheless a strong flier. The muscles of its pectoral girdle are well developed. The pronounced "keel" on its sternum, called the carina, serves to anchor these powerful flight muscles.

Owl bones, like the bones of most birds, are light and pneumatic, but they are far from weak. Though mostly hollow, they are crossbraced by scores of solid shafts attached to opposite sides of their inner wall, giving them strength without adding appreciably to their weight.

The skeleton of an owl is a sturdy structure that contains and protects the internal organs. It also serves as a solid but flexible foundation for the flight feathers of wings and tail, as well as an anchor for the bird's lethal legs and feet—its business end.

The muscles and tendons of foreleg and foot are especially powerful and

A great gray owlet's needle-sharp talons.

efficient. The illustration below shows the grasping equipment of a typical large owl. Flexor muscles are so structured that a marmot or hare hapless enough to be gripped by the owl's claws will only tighten their hold the more frantically it struggles to escape.

The legs of an owl are typically short. One exception is the barn owl, a bird that hunts over open grasslands and relies heavily on hearing. Like a harrier, it glides and tilts above the ground with longish legs dangling, talons open and ready for action. Thus equipped, the barnie can swoop down and snatch a mouse without getting entangled in tall grass.

Another exception is the burrowing owl. The billy owl is a classic cursorial bird (one that runs about on open ground), like the Roadrunner of cartoon fame. The burrowing owl shares with the latter a fondness for beetles and snakes—and longish legs with little or no feathering.

The talons at the tips of the toes of most owls are exceptionally long, strong, and sharp. They are especially impressive in the great horned owl, heavyweight of bird hunters. Few animals ever survive the onslaught of those claws. Combined with the power of the tendons and muscles to which they are joined,

ANATOMY OF TALON-LOCKING MECHANISM

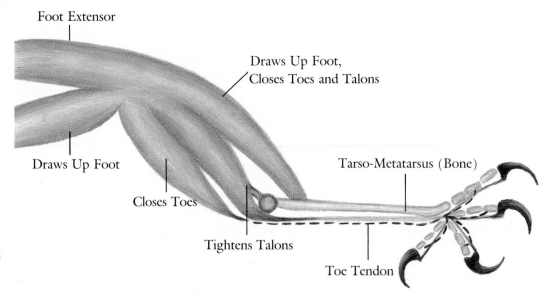

Foot Extensor

Draws Up Foot, Closes Toes and Talons

Draws Up Foot

Closes Toes

Tightens Talons

Tarso-Metatarsus (Bone)

Toe Tendon

(Drawing based on Heinrich, 1987; by permission of Princeton University Press.)

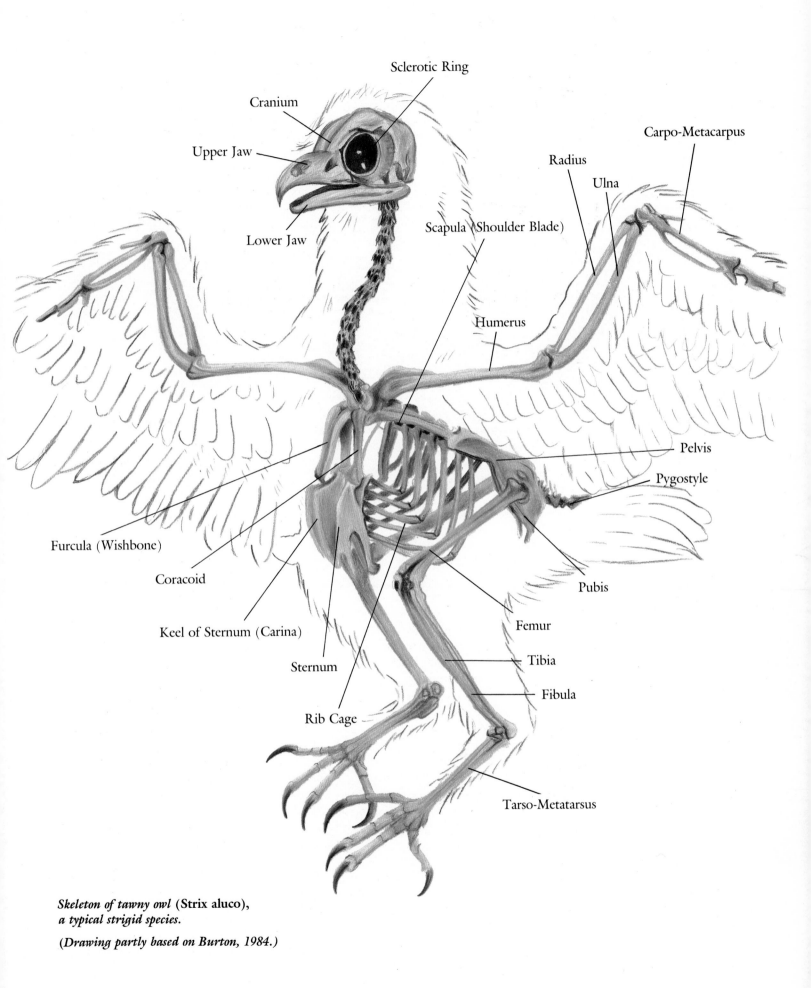

Skeleton of tawny owl (**Strix aluco**),
a typical strigid species.

(**Drawing partly based on Burton, 1984.**)

A juvenile burrowing owl exercises its wings, strengthening its wing muscles for its first attempts at flight.

they can snap the neck of a groundhog or baby lamb as if it were a toothpick.*

A unique anatomical peculiarity of the owl is its extraordinarily flexible neck. From earliest times people have been amused and mesmerized by the ability these birds have to rotate their heads in what seems to be a full circle. This is the source of the myth that one can get rid of an owl by walking around it: the owl will keep staring at you, its head will keep turning, its neck will twist into a braid, and eventually the bird will choke.

What is, of course, the case is that an owl can almost swivel its head 180 degrees to right or left. It can also turn its face completely upside down, crown facing the ground, chin to the sky. It can even flip back its entire head, so that the feathers of forehead and crown wedge in between and blend with the scapular (shoulder) feathers and the plumage of the upper back. And it can crane its head sideways in a vast number of crazy, comical ways.

What allows the owl to do this are seven extra cervical, or neck, vertebrae that are not fused. This loose articulation, coupled with strong and supple muscles, allows the owl an almost unlimited number of angles at which it may direct its facial disks.

Facial disks are what make an owl look like an owl. They are also the centerpieces of the owl's eyes and ears. Facial disks are therefore an indispensable part of what it is to be an owl. They are an essential feature of owlish anatomy.

Basically, they function as a set of dish antennae. Like the dish of a paraboloid reflector, the concave surfaces of an owl's facial disks concentrate sounds. The feathers of these disks, particularly at the edges, are specially modified to function as sound receptors. Edge feathers not only trap sound, they are exceptionally mobile and are imbedded in flaps of flexible tissue that constitute the highly directional outer rim of the bird's external ears.

The disks, moreover, frame the eyes. They focus our attention irresistibly on two of the owl's most outstanding faculties: sight and hearing.

---

* Let this be a warning to any Samaritan who may be tempted to rescue an owlet floundering about apparently helplessly on the ground. Many owlets, including those of the great horned variety, spend longish periods on the forest floor before developing full flight capability. Papa and mama owl are certain to be watching you, quite ready to plunge those talons into *your* withers—with disastrous effects on both your anatomy and your altruism.

VISION

The eyes of an owl are built for gathering light. This does not mean they have low resolving power; the ability to see an image sharply is probably as developed in an owl as it is in any kind of bird, including the hawk. Also, like a hawk or an eagle, an owl can see clearly at a remarkable distance.

Contrary to popular opinion, owls can and often do use their vision in broad daylight. Sometimes an owl will scan the sky for hawks that might try to rob it of its prey. More often it will keep a sharp lookout simply because it knows that hawks and falcons have a nasty habit of mobbing members of the owl clan. Many a hawk watcher armed with powerful binoculars has been astounded by the ability of a nearby owl to detect soaring hawks even before the watcher has had an inkling of tiny specks floating about in the blue. So much for the notion that owls are blinded by daylight.

Still, it is for nocturnal vision that the strixine eye is specially adapted. It is a huge eye. Were ours as big in proportion to our body weight we would look like goggle-eyed science fiction monsters. The owl's outsize eyes are dramatically placed, facing forward in the center of the flat or slightly concave facial disks and well above the bill so that the latter will not impinge upon their visual field. The degree of binocularity, or three-dimensional vision, achieved by owls is higher than that of any other group of birds.

Eye Structure and Function

When an owl is about to feed its young, a grayish white membrane quickly travels across the cornea, making the eye look milky. This is the third eyelid, or nictitating membrane (to nictitate simply means to wink). Many birds and reptiles have third eyelids. In no group is this feature more developed than in owls. The winking membrane is opaque and tough and protects the eye in various ways: it lubricates the surface; it shields the eye against glare; and above all, it protects it from an inadvertent peck from a hungry owlet—as well as a not-so-inadvertent lunge by a rival owl or another predator.

Owl eyes are fixed in their sockets, or virtually so. A great amount of space is taken up by the internal ocular cavity. The correlation between seeing and hearing—the owl's eyes are almost dead center in the paraboloid disk that is its basic sound receptor—is extraordinary, a synchronous eye-ear balance. With outsize eye sockets and huge ear openings combined in one optical-acoustic cavity, the

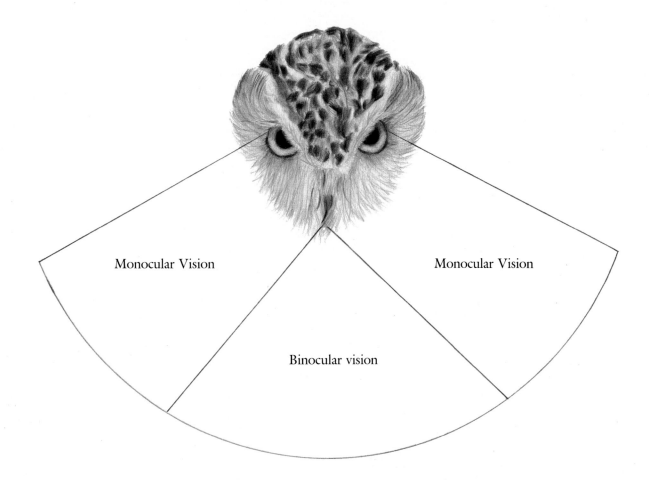

Monocular Vision

Monocular Vision

Binocular vision

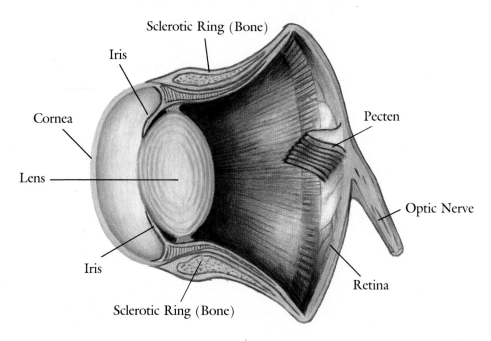

Sclerotic Ring (Bone)

Iris

Cornea

Pecten

Lens

Optic Nerve

Iris

Retina

Sclerotic Ring (Bone)

(Adapted from Burton, 1955.)

need for firm anchorage in a rigid helmet of solid bone is obvious. However, the owl's helmet is highly flexible. Thanks to specialized neck bones and muscles, the head can be moved in almost any direction at great speed—and, the pupil of each eye can be individually controlled. Thus, a flying owl can swivel its head from side to side while the iris of each eye expands or contracts differentially in response to the varying light intensities of different features in the landscape. Simultaneously, of course, the ears of the bird can make analogous adjustments to the changing features of the sound spectrum. Combine these capabilities with silent flight and razor-sharp claws and you have a passport to eternity for foolhardy mice.

The Retina: Rods and Cones

Internally the most important feature of the owl's eye is the retina. Two kinds of light-sensitive cells are found in all retinal membranes: rods and cones. These cells, called photoreceptors, work in different ways. Cones are essentially responsible for color discrimination. Rods respond chiefly to light intensity. Both contribute to sharpness of image or, in optician's jargon, resolution. Rods contain a special pigment called rhodopsin, or visual purple, which is extraordinarily sensitive to the minutest amount of light. Indeed, rods are the cells that spring into action as we stargaze, gradually improving our capacity to register details in the dark. Our so-called peripheral vision is due to the photosensitivity of the

rods in our retinas. Predictably, owl retinas are rich in rods, and these rods are simply loaded with rhodopsin. Cones are by no means absent, but they are far less numerous in an owl than they are in a pigeon, a bird in which color perception is highly developed. Not surprisingly, diurnal owls like the burrowing owl have more cones than nocturnal ones. Experiments with burrowing owls have shown that this species can differentiate among a fair number of colors.

Most owls do see some color, perhaps a bit more than the ordinary house cat, whose world is essentially composed of whites, blacks, and grays. Still, the world as seen by an owl is very much like that seen by a cat, giving further credence to the description of an owl as a cat with wings.

Night Vision

Just how well does an owl see in the dark? There are, believe it or not, detailed dissertations designed to prove that the optical faculties of an owl at night are not really much better than ours. These learned treatises are in the same category as such proofs that bumblebees cannot fly—a scientist "demonstrated" that it was aerodynamically impossible—or that on the basis of their metabolism ruby-throated hummingbirds cannot possibly travel across the Gulf of Mexico, an impossibility recklessly disregarded by the thousands of ruby-throats that do exactly that each year.

Actually, in total darkness an owl will see nothing. But add a tiny bit of light and remarkable things happen. Long ago L. R. Dice showed that long-eared owls could see dead prey (freshly killed mice) up to six feet away at a level of illumination of 0.00000073 foot candles. (A foot candle is the illumination produced by a standard candle at a distance of one foot.) More recently J. Lindblad has shown that long-eareds do even better than that: they can find dead prey at ten feet at 0.00000016 foot candles. To put this in perspective, a long-eared owl trapped in the Astrodome would probably be able to find a stationary mouse with just one candle lit in the center of the arena.

However, the owl might have trouble seeing the mouse if it was belly down, and therefore lighter colored, rather than belly up. Back color blends with leaves and soil, making it harder for the owl to locate the food. Many experiments have shown that when presented with live prey of different colors, owls will typically choose those whose hue does not match the available background.

HEARING

If the owl's eyesight is exemplary, its hearing is one of the marvels of nature. Indeed, it is a whole book of marvels to which almost every month, it seems, a new and exciting chapter is added.

In recent years most of these chapters have been or are being written by Eric Knudsen and Mark Konishi, brilliant neurobiologists working with a cohort of gifted colleagues.

But a remarkable opening chapter was penned just over two decades ago by Roger Payne, best known today for his pioneering recordings of whale songs. In a series of elegant experiments Payne demonstrated the startling fact that barn owls can hunt with almost 100 percent efficiency when they can see nothing at all. Simply by tracking the sound produced by the padding of tiny feet the barnie can zero in on a moving mouse and cup its talons around the mouse's body. Over and over again Payne's owls performed this feat of flying in pitch-black darkness, scooping up their locomotive meals with unerring accuracy.

If the owl's hearing was unimpaired, it usually got its mouse on the first try. If its ears were plugged so as to reduce its hearing ability by half, it might miss the mouse on the first swoop, but then the owl would swing around, aim its facial disks at the moving target, swoop down a second time, and claim its prize. Remarkably, this shows that the bird is able to make instant adjustments to sudden alterations in its spectrum of perceived sound with scarcely any lessening of its ability to procure food by ear power alone.

A World of Sounds

Owls live in a world of sounds we can barely imagine. Their ears respond to rustles and squeaks the way a bloodhound's nose responds to scents. It has been said that the range of frequencies owls can perceive is more limited than our own, and some species of owls probably cannot hear the very lowest pitches as well as we can. Still, the hoots of the great gray owl are almost as deep as the booming of the spruce grouse, the lowest-pitched sound produced by a North American bird. And the territorial song of the male barred owl is nothing if not a rich, reverberating bass. But arguments as to the hearing range of owls miss the point; an explanation of the phenomenon of owl hearing lies elsewhere.

Acoustic Maps

A number of years ago Knudsen and Konishi began to ask themselves questions about barn owls. As one of these heart-faced wraiths zigzags through total darkness, tilting its head from side to side as it focuses on the movements of a scurrying mouse, what actually goes on inside its brain? Can the owl "print" and recall mouse pathways that are used repeatedly? Can it erase a memory when it clearly is no longer useful, and can it then log in new or replacement patterns? Can it identify different animals by their sounds? How does it compensate for the welter of ambient noises always present in nature? How does weather influence sound detection hunting (wet leaves don't crinkle as nicely as dry ones)? These and a myriad of other questions were to serve as the basis for a series of illuminating experiments detailed in articles that can only be summarized here.

At the outset, Knudsen succeeded in tracing the neural paths of the acoustic stimuli actually recorded in the barn owl's brain. The movement of an animal scuttling about in a natural environment creates a three-dimensional pattern. Knudsen and Konishi found that as a sequence of acoustic stimuli was received, a three-dimensional grid would build up in the brain of the owl exactly corresponding to the pattern created by the moving animal. And, they found that this grid along with others, like computer memories, can be

Tiny ear tufts appeared on this northern pygmy owl as a passing flock of chickadees discovered its perch, a seldom seen defense pose probably never before recorded photographically.

stored, discarded, altered, or replaced according to changing needs.

Even more remarkable than the owl's ability to record a number of movement patterns, the neurobiologists found, is its ability to acoustically scan and learn the features of the hunting area. Here's how this works. In addition to the territories owls defend at nesting time from interlopers of their own species, most owls that survive to maturity develop a home range, an extended foraging area that they work over systematically throughout the year as they develop a sense of the landscape. The acoustic features of the terrain—echo effects in domes of dense foliage, crackling noises in grassy spots, the slurpy sounds of a boggy border, the dry swish of sand and gravel—gradually intermingle with a growing awareness of the noises produced by the different creatures inhabiting that landscape. This awareness includes a sense of seasonal variations (voles, a key owl food, are nocturnal in summer, diurnal in winter); of the difference between autogenous sounds, such as the courting bleat of Fowler's toad, and incidental sounds, like the swish of a garter snake through sand; and of the effects of weather on the sonic spectrum—barn owls demonstrably

hunt less efficiently after a heavy rain.

Taking all the foregoing into consideration and factoring in longevity and cumulative learning, what emerges is an animal—the barn owl—with the astounding ability to build, retain, and modify a detailed map of its home turf—an acoustic map, to be sure, but one probably overlaid with a visual memory of the features of the same region.

What is especially important about Knudsen and Konishi's findings is that these abilities of the barn owl seem to a greater or lesser degree to be shared by all species of owls. Clearly the more nocturnal species, such as the long-eared and the boreal, will be found to possess greater aural acuity—and therefore more detailed acoustic maps—than essentially eye-oriented day hunters like the burrowing and the pygmy owls.

Something now must be added on the key topic of identification by sound, a critical element in the building of an acoustic map.

Sound Discrimination

Great birders are known for their ability to pick out hundreds of bird species by song or even by chip notes. If owls could talk, they'd make the best sound-birder look pretty bad. These superbly aurally equipped animals can and do learn to differentiate a whole universe of animal and ambient sounds—and to act accordingly. Without looking beyond his own backyard experiments, the present writer can confidently assert that great horned owls easily tell apart by call rabbits, raccoons, and skunks; screech, barred, and long-eared owls; red-tailed and red-shouldered hawks; pheasants and chickens; ducks and geese, not to mention dogs and cats and the great horned's relentless arch enemy, the common crow. Great horned owls will also quickly react to anything that even hints of a snake in the grass, being both snake eaters and snake prey.

But for an owl to make a living, the refinements of sound discrimination must go much further. A fox with cubs barks; rabbits go hopping through briers; a startled doe crashes through a thicket; gophers crawl through burrows; untold hundreds of mice, voles, and shrews go scuttling through leaf litter and pine needles. And as a backdrop to all this there is wind, rain, thunder, falling branches, airplanes, braying donkeys, and the ubiquitous baying of suburban hounds. Konishi's research supports the view that a healthy barn owl can and indeed does sort through this welter of noises and learns to focus with extraordinary acuity on the sounds belonging to creatures that are good to eat and to avoid or ignore other sounds.

The Ears of Owls

The foundation of the wonderful hearing just described is a pair of ears that for size and sensitivity are unmatched in any other group of birds and, among terrestrial animals, are probably equaled only by human ears. (The hearing of marine mammals approaches mythic dimensions; sperm whales are said to be able to hear each other across entire oceans!)

In most birds the external ear is a small round opening. Owls have long vertical slits, sometimes as deep as the head itself. The outer rims of the facial disks are fringed with feathers highly specialized to conduct sound. These border the ear openings and are complemented by flaps of skin in front and/or in back of the ear conch. Sometimes called opercular flaps, they are very mobile and can expand, contract, or adjust the angle of the ear opening.

All this equipment the owl uses in scanning its terrain in much the same way that a cat scans by rotating its ears. (The so-called ears of "eared owls" are erectile feather tufts that apparently play a role in courtship display and camouflage but have nothing to do with hearing.)

HEAD OF SNOWY OWLS SHOWING EXTERNAL EAR
Ruff of facial disk raised to reveal position of ear opening.

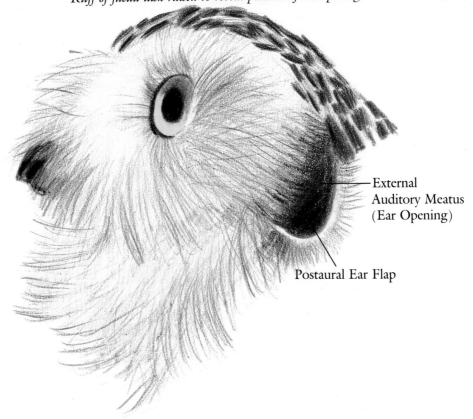

External
Auditory Meatus
(Ear Opening)

Postaural Ear Flap

(Drawing partly after Mikkola, 1983.)

Above: The skull of a great horned owl. Far right: Detail of screech owl wing feathers.

A distinctive feature in the ears of many owls is asymmetry. In these birds one of the external ear cavities is placed much higher than the other. This asymmetric positioning is most pronounced in the boreal owl, a species noted for sound-dependent hunting. Not surprisingly, the ears of great gray owls—the "snow plungers" that can hear a field vole running under two feet of hard-packed snow—are also asymmetric, as are those of the barn owl, past master of hunting by ear power.

Asymmetry works by enhancing the depth perception involved in typical binaural hearing. Konishi has shown that exact localization of sounds by barn owls is achieved by measuring the difference in the time it takes the sound to reach each ear. Typically, this amounts to no more than 150 microseconds (a microsecond is a millionth of a second), a short span indeed. Konishi's experiments nonetheless indicate that owls can detect a time lag as minuscule as ten microseconds.

Konishi hypothesizes that the owl uses differences in sound intensity to distinguish the vertical from the horizontal displacement of a sound source. This done, the owl will lower its head until the level of sound is equally loud in both ears, and at that moment the source of the sound will be in line with the eyes of the owl.

Ear asymmetry, however, is not essential for all species. Many owls have ears that are quite symmetrically placed and evidently hear very well indeed. The great horned is one of them. Nonetheless, the most finely tuned acoustic receptor equipment—huge facial disks, very mobile dermal flaps, an exceptionally large ear conch and external ear cavity, as well as pronounced skull asymmetry—are encountered in nocturnal forest hunters such as the boreal and great gray owls, whose dependence on sound for survival is obvious.

Their great eyes peering intently, facial disks flexing to catch the faintest rustle, owls rely on special plumage patterns to make them invisible when pounce-hunting from a perch and on unique feather structures to render flight as noiseless as possible when hunting on the wing.

These peculiarities of plumage are our next subject.

SKULL OF BOREAL OWL

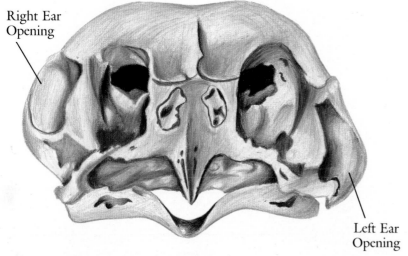

Right Ear Opening

Left Ear Opening

Note the asymmetrical placement of the ear openings, which enhances depth perception in an owl's hearing. (Drawing partly after Burton, 1984.)

Feather Colors and Patterns

The color repertoire of owl feathers is not spectacular. But the palette of shades is extraordinary: all the tints of black and white; a grand array of grays—ash, slate, pearl, taupe; the full spectrum of browns—buffs and ochres, sienna, chestnut, cinnamon, russet, and fawn.

Nature has arranged these hues in a kaleidoscope of shapes, both crisp and blurry: streaks, stripes, and bars; wedges, carets, and arrowheads; stippling, speckling, and the dappled effect of dots on shoulders, napes, and backs—the whole in an amazing variety of contours.

These contours in turn fall into webworks of wavy, wormlike markings and crosshatched lattices of lines admirably designed to conceal the bird when it is at rest—the welter of patterns commonly referred to as cryptic plumage. These patterns are masterpieces of mimicry; their functional efficiency is spectacular, their beauty subtle.

Not a few species show startling configurations on the facial disks, forehead, beak, chin, or upper breast. These are often in the form of moustaches or beards, V-shaped frontal shields, or exaggerated edges to the facial disks. These designs are thought to be an aid in intimidating prey by enhancing the owl's ferocious mien.

This is certainly true from a human point of view when one thinks of the effect on one's nerves of a glowering great horned owl. However, one can easily extend this point of view too far. It is certainly doubtful that any mouse has ever been intimidated by the frontal T of a saw-whet owl or by the raised "eyebrows" of the boreal owl. In the saw-whet the flash mark merely enhances the cuteness of the Acadian Adorable, as Jonathan Maslow has so fittingly dubbed this bird; the eyebrows of the boreal just give it a look of perpetual surprise. Apparently, the chief function of these facial flash marks is to enable members of a family group to recognize each other in the dark. In the case of cavity nesters, many of which have young with vivid patches of white on the face, the marks aid parent birds entering the cavity to locate nestlings under light conditions even poorer than those of the ambient night.

It is well known that individual facial marks in swans, as well as pelage patterns in gorillas, serve as name tags, enabling members of a flock or extended family to locate and recog-

Left: The wing feathers of the great horned owl show the fluted edges that make silent flight possible for this bird.

nize each other. It is not farfetched to suppose that subtle differences in the white moustache-like streaks of great gray owls, for example, serve a similar function among these birds, which have the peculiarity of assembling in loose colonies in especially favored areas.

Countershading

Countershading is an adaptation for concealment found widely in the animal world. In birds, light-hued plumage on the underparts is matched by dark feathering above. The contrast enables birds that live in open country to take full advantage of the interplay of light and shadow to remain inconspicuous against grassy, rocky, sandy, or pebbly backgrounds. Among the most striking examples of evolutionary adaptation is the fact that countershading in woodland owls, which hunt at night, is typically faint and in many cases nonexistent, but is well developed in burrowing and short-eared owls, diurnal hunters, the former of which permanently live in, while the latter habitually roam over, barren grounds, prairies, and stubble fields.

Silent Flight

Perhaps no feature of owl feathering is more unique than the one illustrated in the drawing of a barn owl wing (below) and Art Wolfe's photographs of great horned owl feathers (left).

In a hawk or a pigeon, the outer rim of a flight feather—the one that propels the bird forward on the downstroke—is stiff; when the bird "steps on the gas" the noise made by its wings can be quite startling. Anyone who has heard a flock of pigeons take off or put up a grouse while hiking in the woods knows how loud feathers in full swing can be.

Any owl whose wings made such a racket would soon die of starvation. Thanks to serrated feather edges, such misfortune need not occur. The wing comes down, the air flows smoothly through the indentations, and the owl buoyantly and silently slips through the trees or quarters over the meadow, facial disks shifting to catch every rustle, twin telephoto eyes scanning the ground for the faintest twitch, ready to zero in on shrew, mole, or mouse. And, of course, the yummy little beastie will have no inkling of the owl's approach.

WING OF A COMMON BARN OWL

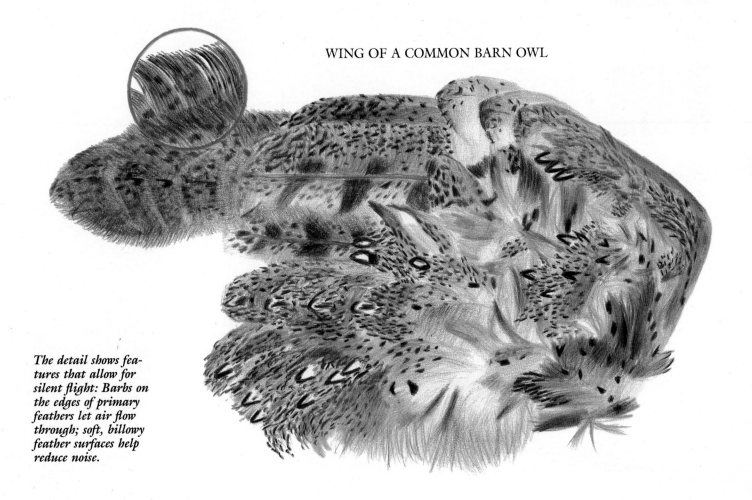

The detail shows features that allow for silent flight: Barbs on the edges of primary feathers let air flow through; soft, billowy feather surfaces help reduce noise.

*Above and right: A
screech owl in flight.*

The silent downstroke of an owl's wing
does not just result from the open outer edge.
The entire surface of the wing as well as of
body contour feathers is soft and billowy. The
trailing edge of the wing does not, in fact, feel
at all like a flight feather, but more like the
downy plumes on the breast of a brooding
hen.

In the evolution of noiseless flight the economy of nature is evident. Only true night
hunters possess these specialized plumes. Day-
fliers, like the pygmy owls and the burrowing
owl, rely primarily on speed and vision and
have flight feathers that are quite conventional.

Color Phases

Bird listers scanning the sky of southern Florida for a glimpse of the rare short-tailed hawk know that it comes in two color variants, a dark and a light, so different that a tyro could be forgiven for believing them to be different birds.

It was assuredly not tyros, however, who classified the two color morphs of the snow goose into separate species for more than a century. We know today that the dark form—the "blue goose" of yesteryear—is just a color variant occurring in mixed clutches with the white.

Chromatic variability hardly stops with hawks and geese. Many owls show it, none more strikingly than certain members of the screech owl complex.

Screech owls in the East come in two colors, gray and red. The latter is really a tone much like that of a red fox. These chromatic variants are often referred to as color phases, a misleading word since it implies transience, whereas the presence of red and gray birds in a mixed brood is almost certainly genetically determined.

Technically, the phenomenon is known as dichromatism. It shows up in western screech owls as well, but more rarely. In western birds either gray or brown tends to predominate. In both East and West exquisitely detailed variations in feathering appear from race to race in response to varying vegetational patterns and other ecological factors. These variant plumages have been studied in admirable detail by Joe T. Marshall, Jr.

Many explanations have been proposed to account for the rich rufous owls so often found in eastern woodlands. Marshall's own hypothesis is perhaps the most cogent of all. It goes like this:

A. Eastern forests feature an extraordinary density of deciduous trees. For sheer variety of species, few spots on the globe equal, and none surpasses, the foothills of the southern Appalachians. Furthermore, the kaleidoscope of greens, yellows, reds, and browns that brightens Appalachian valleys and hillsides from Georgia to the Gaspé is simply unknown in the West.

B. Screech owls reach their maximum vulnerability to predation in late summer and autumn.*

C. Significantly, it is in early fall that screech owls develop their most distinctive and characteristic plumage.† It therefore follows that maximum degree of camouflage is directly related to maximum predator pressure.

But let's look at the matter in another way. Most of the carnivores likely to attack screech owls are color-blind—or nearly so. These include other species of owls. (See Vision, page 139, for color perception in owls.) Reddish plumage enhances the effectiveness of cryptic markings. Color-blind predators do distinguish a broad palette of shades. Thus color-blindness is not a conclusive argument against what may yet prove to be the best explanation of dichromatism. But it is a muffler of sorts, and it must be considered in the context of other reservations. For instance, for the hypothesis to be fully confirmed it would be necessary to prove that red owls tend to roost in reddish foliage, at least during periods of high vulnerability, and that gray owls favor the immediacy of gray bark or the cover of dense evergreens.

Several tomes might be filled with the results of investigations aimed at proving or disproving such behavior. Indeed the gray-red dichromatism of eastern screech owls could be explained teleologically as a conundrum of nature designed to keep Ph.D. candidates from running out of dissertation material.

The fact is that there is considerable overlap in roosting behavior. In early fall gray owls are often seen flying about and perching on the outer branches of deciduous trees. Red owls, conversely, frequently roost in conifers or in knotholes of gray-barked trees. One red owl, a large, handsome female, has lived for at least eight years within an isolated pine grove in Stamford, Connecticut. This stand of pines, two to three acres in extent, from which the owl seldom strays, is separated from other similar stands by tracts of open oak, maple, and beech woodland that should be irresistible to a red owl. But there it is! My red-phase friend refuses to oblige the scientists and is

An adult screech owl in a white pine.

---

* During the nesting season there seems to be a mechanism that renders screech owls less vulnerable to predators. This may partly be because their natural enemies are busy rearing their own young, which would lead them to concentrate their hunting on easy and abundant quarry. Preying on other predators is not a high-yield strategy.

† Ignorance of this fact caused much confusion in the early classification of screech owls; the collectors of yesteryear typically shot and mounted nesting adults in frayed plumage.

only too delighted to stay in its condominium of deep dark pines.

Two more facts about dichromatism, and then we are done. One concerns an experiment that merits discussion because of its source. No less an authority than Ealon Eaton claims to have converted gray-phase owls to red-phase owls by feeding them a diet of shrimp! This, of course, is simply an instance of artificially induced erythrism, or reddening of fur or feathers, by the deposition—in this case contrived—of pigments known as carotenoids. It is well known that captive flamingoes and scarlet ibises soon lose their bright red hues and that these can be quickly restored by mixing in shrimp or other arthropods high in carotene with their food.

The other fact is that eastern screech owls frequently show intermediate plumages, in both color and shape of markings. As any New England owler knows, it is hardly rare to call out screech owls that are neither red nor gray. Mixed broods are instructive. In one such group three gray owls showed vermiculations (wavy, ribbonlike markings) across breast and belly and one showed chestnut reticulations (a webwork of wide-mesh quadrangles). In one well-known captive bird, the feathering of the foreparts (frontal half of the "ears," facial disks, chest, flanks, belly, vent, undertail area) is that of a classic gray owl. The back of the bird is an amazing, beautiful burnt gold, from the back of the ear tufts, crown, nape, and mantle all the way to the rump and upper side of the tail feathers. Nature, as William James said, is Gothic, not classical. Anything goes, just as long as it isn't a clear disadvantage to survival.

Thus, the best explanation of these color phases may be that there really is none. Nature is an extravagant spendthrift. It keeps tinkering with old models and inventing new ones with reckless abandon. Inventions that do not work are quickly weeded out. Ones that do are retained and often elaborated upon until limiting factors curb further refinements. Often these refinements include modifications that are only semifunctional or embellishments that neither impair nor improve the status of a species. The dichromatism of eastern screech owls seems to partake of this character.

DIGESTION *Owl Pellets*

Owls, if they can, bolt their food whole. Mice go down in one or two gulps, bones, fur, and all. Larger prey like a rabbit or a woodrat must first be broken up into bite-size chunks. Still, what an owl considers bite-size can be surprisingly large.

As anyone who has raised chickens knows, three-week-old pullets are pretty big. The writer once fed four such young chicks to a great horned owl. *Bubo* quickly swallowed the first three, head first. The fourth took longer to get down. Its legs and feet dangled for a minute out of the big owl's mouth, while the needed room was being created in its belly. What was going on inside the owl was a process called pellet formation.

In a sac called the ventriculus, digestive juices and muscular contractions actually liquefy the digestible portion of the owl's meal. Fur, bone, bills, claws, teeth, feathers, insect fragments, and all manner of similar indigestible solids collect at the bottom of the pouch. There they are churned into a pellet, or casting, which the owl eventually regurgitates. An owl coughing up a pellet looks like a cat coughing up a hair ball.

Owl pellets vary in size, color, and consistency depending on the species of owl and the nature of its meal. Snails, earthworms, and beetles, often the only food available to a barn owl on a rainy night, yield tight little brown pellets. Large, fluffy, grayish castings are produced by the liquefaction of Norway rats. In this type of pellet the teeth and bones are imbedded in soft fur.

The regurgitated remains of an owl's meal are almost always excellently preserved. This is not the case with the castings of falcons and hawks; their potent digestive enzymes dissolve bones far more efficiently than the milder gastric juices of owls.

Owl pellets often accumulate in specific areas. The great horned owl, an omnivorous species, regularly carries its catch to a "chopping block," usually a broad limb, where the prey is dismembered and eaten at leisure; the pellets collect underneath. Screech owls, also omnivorous, eat most of what they catch on the spot; they do, however, fly off to traditional roosting spots, where the pellets that have been developing in the meantime tend to be regurgitated.

Owl pellets are excellent indicators of the food habits of different species. This is especially useful to the field ecologist interested in unraveling the dynamics of predator-prey interactions. Since owls are superlative hunters the contents of their castings are very valuable to zoologists studying the fauna of a particular locality. Small mammals, in particular, can be elusive and difficult to survey. In one well-known instance a new species was added to a local checklist by a providential pellet; a barn owl living in a belfry in Middletown, Connecticut, provided the first tangible evidence of red-backed pine mice in the area. More recently a new gerbil was discovered in southwest Africa through its remains in an owl pellet.

Strange facts about animal behavior can be gleaned from owl pellets. Barn owls, for example, do not crawl into the tunnels of moles to ferret out these plump beasties; yet moles turn up regularly in barn owl castings. And in one Old World study cited by Sparks and Soper, moles made up nearly half of the diet of tawny owls from May to October. Evidently, these "velvet diggers" mine the surface or poke about the leaf litter far more often than the average gardener would be inclined to believe.

But perhaps the most fascinating use of owl pellets involves the reconstruction of extinct faunas. Fossil pellets are often well preserved in caves where owls have dwelled. Such caves—where the fossil remains of Pleistocene animals, including ground sloths and owls, abound—are found in the Caribbean, where the writer was born and raised. Approximately 4,000 years ago, many of these Caribbean islands began for the first time to be colonized by humans, in particular Arawak Indians from the South American mainland. Paleontologist David Steadman of the Smithsonian Institution has ascertained, through the analysis of fossil owl pellets, that 33 percent of the small birds and mammals on the island of Antigua became extinct almost immediately after the Arawaks arrived.

It is well known that large animals are very sensitive to human intrusion. Because of this, the massive die-offs of large continental mammals at the end of the Pleistocene era were once attributed to the activities of the recently arrived Indians. This particular theory was subsequently challenged, and the more prevalent explanation of the extinctions became dramatic climatic change. But the new evidence from owl pellets, of all things, suggests that the human animal may have been the major cause of the huge Pleistocene die-offs after all.

8

OWL BEHAVIOR
Variations on a Theme

Left: Barred owl in nesting cavity drying its feathers; these birds are fond of bathing. Right: Burrowing owl preening itself.

*E*thology is the science that deals with how animals behave in their natural surroundings. Those who pursue this line of study must be as unobtrusive as possible. The best ethologist would be silent, odorless, and invisible. To study owls he would also have to be able to see in the dark.

This is a roundabout way of explaining why knowledge of owl behavior in nature—strixine ethology—has enormous gaps. What we do not know (and would very much like to) could fill a book fifty times as big as this one. In ornithology, study of how and why owls behave as they do is one of the last genuine frontiers. Nonetheless, patience, perseverance, hardiness, and a dash of creativity on the part of owl observers have contributed a degree of understanding of what owls do for a living.

A few interesting examples of owl behavior will be presented here. They are largely based on the author's observations.

COURTSHIP: A Primer of Strixine Gallantry

Great Horned Owl

To those whose ears and heart are finely attuned to the pulse of the seasons, the hooting of the great horned owl is the true harbinger of spring. In much of its range it is the earliest breeder among the birds. Pair formation often begins in early winter. An unmated male will start the ritual by choosing a suitable nesting site. Ideally, the spot will have a proper ready-built nest that the suitor can offer to a potential bride; in particular, the site will also present ample opportunities for long-term hunting.

The propertied male announces his availability—each evening at dusk and each morning before dawn, he pours out owlish desire in a throbbing bass. When the moon is full, his hooting may be heard the whole night long.

If he is lucky, an unattached female will pause to check him out, not neglecting at the same time to take a critical peek at the apartment he is offering with such noisy pride.

If both he and his choice of real estate meet with her approval, courtship begins in earnest. This is a slow, ponderous, solemn rite. Its most notable feature is long and elaborate vocalizations. Antiphonal dueting—call-pause-call—will often go on for a month or more. In the Northeast these bouts of amorous booming start in December and reach a peak in January and February.

As courtship nears climax, the duets grow in intensity. Pauses between calls get shorter and shorter. Eventually the calls overlap. Contrapuntal calling is proof positive of a fully formed pair bond.

The consummation of all this amorous activity generally results in the production of two, more rarely three, pure white eggs. These are laid in January in the nest, which, as previously noted, is often the abandoned homestead of a red-tailed hawk. In unforested mountainous regions, the nest is often little more than a scrape on a ledge.

Incubation, by the female alone, can last over a month. During that time she is fed by the male, all the while stoutly facing the vagaries of winter weather.

The owlets usually hatch by mid-February. For the first three weeks of life, they are almost constantly brooded by the mother owl. A great horned owl nest with a mother owl spreading a mantle of feathers over two dark-faced balls of fluff while a blizzard rages is a not-to-be-forgotten picture of steadfastness in adversity.

The stately ceremonies of courtship described above follow a rigid pattern that does not allow much leeway for invention. In addition to vocalizations, the pattern includes bill fencing, mutual preening, ritual feeding, and slow elaborate dances in a ritualistic sequence that must be followed step by unimpeded step if the eventual goals of copulation and nidification are to be reached.

The entire process may be considered representative of what is variously referred to as automatic, innate, or encoded behavior. It is a sequential series of commands that seems to be programmed on a computer card or floppy disk imbedded in the brain of the owl. The completion of one step acts as a trigger to the next and so on until the program is exhausted, whereupon either a new program is activated or nonprogrammed aleatory behaviors (such as are necessarily associated with hunting-provisioning) take over.

A single observer is seldom able to witness the entire gamut of such a prolonged scenario. Our conception of the whole is in fact a mosaic of numerous separate observations. It is an imperfect mosaic: many specific stages in the courtship are imperfectly known. Others, such as copulatory behavior, have yet, to my knowledge, to be described.

AN EXTRAORDINARY EVENT

Despite the foregoing, it was the extraordinary privilege of the author and a friend to witness a pair of great horned owls go through what may be described as a complete courtship sequence in a single night.

To appreciate what happened the reader needs to be cognizant of a few facts. The first is that female horned owls are larger and heavier than males. (True for most owls, this is technically referred to as reverse sexual dimorphism.) For a long time many field workers believed the females to be correspondingly deeper-voiced. We now know this is not the case. The male, despite his smaller size, has longer tympanic membranes in his voice box (syrinx) and thus hoots in a lower register.

Secondly, the timetable of courtship is a crucial factor. Birds that begin to feel the mating urge in December and that build a family bond from January through February will have an unimaginable surfeit of hormones if March rolls along and they are still unmated.

This was precisely the case with the owls involved in the incident now to be narrated. Some years ago, the author and a birding companion from the New Haven Bird Club were looking for barred owls. It was a clear,

Great horned owl surveys its domain from a tree stump.

warm night in early March. There was a brilliant full moon, at first somewhat obscured by mist, but as the evening wore on the veil of moisture lifted and the bright lunar light shone through.

We had chosen to begin our foray at Caumsett State Forest, on the Housatonic River. There the river channel has been broadened into a pleasure boating area called Lake Zoar. We were standing on the west shore, facing this area and a forested ridge about half a mile to the east. Directly in front of us was a large open horseshoe of hemlock trees, about fifty feet deep and twenty feet wide, with the arch of the shoe toward the water and the two sides framing us. I heard a horned owl calling from the cliffs to the east. It was a very deep call and I assumed it to be a female. Half in fun, I tried to see if I could get it to fly to us. A squeal and a hoot, and the incredible happened—a huge dark shadow emerged from the mountains, sailed across a quarter mile of moonlit water, and landed in the cusp of the hemlock stand.

The owl began to go through one of the most bizarre sets of antics I have ever seen a wild animal perform. It bowed deeply over and over; it hooted repeatedly, often pausing, tilting its head to right and left and peering intently as though it were trying to find out if its hoots had produced the desired effect. Between hoots, as it peered, it emitted a startling medley of purrs and growls. Not quite prepared for anything like this, I thought I'd try the "pishing" sound so often used by birders to pull sparrows out of the bush. The owl instantly responded with a loud hair-raising squeal while spreading its wings and erecting its tufts to the fullest. I could imagine newspaper headlines about two birders collected the next day in the form of owl pellets.

Then, from a distant ridge to the southwest, we heard a higher-pitched hoot, and suddenly the gigantic silhouette of a female great horned owl was outlined against the western sky. The big bird landed in the left prong of the horseshoe not more than fifteen feet away from us. I now realized that the first owl must be a male.

By then all hell had broken loose. Boy and girl bird had been brought together by a human being, probably the first in history to become a marriage broker to owls. I was rewarded for my services with the spectacle of a two-month courtship ritual compressed into a few minutes.

The long period of antiphonal duetting—which serves first for sexual recognition, second to establish degree of submissiveness, and finally to proclaim a consummated bond—was abbreviated to five minutes of intense vocal outbursts. These took place from the two separate perches, the birds remaining about fifty feet apart.

Next, the female flew cater-corner to the center right of the horseshoe, where she was joined by the male. Remaining a few inches apart, the pair spent several minutes bowing and scraping and praising each other with purring gurgles. Then they drew closer and went into three minutes or so of intense allopreening (mutual preening) accompanied by soft gurgly vocalizations. This entire second stage took another five minutes.

The birds then began an astonishing slow progression from limb to limb along the right edge of the horseshoe toward the cusp, around it, and then along the left side. At each of approximately six spots they stopped, faced each other, and rotated their bodies slowly on an imaginary vertical axis. At the same time they embraced each other by lifting their wings and overlapping them as if they were laying shingles, lifting and overlapping them again. The term "shingle dance" suggested itself on the spot.

This terpsichorean intimacy lasted another five minutes. Copulation then took place approximately halfway down the left side of the horseshoe. There was, of course, no chance for the precopulatory ritual feeding so often mentioned in the literature. The act itself was predictable. The female chose a limb about ten feet below the crown of a forty-foot hemlock and faced toward the water. The male had some difficulty mounting her since the branch directly overhead did not provide much clearance for the combined bulk of two massive birds. He was therefore obliged to go through quite a bit of squirming and vigorous clapping of his huge wings before he could establish a secure foothold on the back of his mate. At one moment as he flapped his wings, he struck a sleeping chickadee, which fled in mortal terror. It was not easy to time the duration of cloacal apposition;* probably it did not last more than fifteen seconds.

This sequence would have been memorable enough had it been performed only once, but these lusty owls were on to a good thing and not about to let it go.

They separated, flew back to their original perches, and repeated the entire ritual a sec-

* In most birds fertilization is accomplished by the passing of semen from one external opening (cloaca) into another; in copulation both openings are pressed against each other. Hence the term "cloacal apposition."

Brushy rise near den entrance affords these burrowing owls an excellent view.

ond time. Another fifteen minutes of hooting, allopreening, and shingle dancing. But no observers of owl antics have ever been more stunned than the author and his friend when, upon completion of their second performance, the two Lake Zoar owls separated and staged their amorous drama a *third* time! The writer recalls saying: "This is just to make sure I get the sequence right!"

The mating sequence just described is a fair, if speeded-up, example of ritual behavior in owls. The separate steps—often elaborately described and individually named—seem to unfold according to a pattern. In forest-dwelling owls these rites rely heavily on vocal signals. For open country birds, such as the short-eared owl, visual elements predominate. (Our portrait of the short-eared gives a cap-

sule picture of the courtship of this marsh-dwelling owl.) Another well-documented visual behavior of open country–dwelling owls is the angel-wing dance that male snowy owls perform around prospective mates.

All of these behaviors share the feature of appearing to be programmed. There seems to be relatively little that the birds can do to alter them, except perhaps to speed them up as our March-mating Lake Zoar owls were apparently goaded into doing to prevent a hormonal aneurysm.

But owls are also capable of a large variety of nonprogrammed aleatory or problem-solving activities—what might be called owlish wisdom at work. The most obvious of these, of course, is hunting.

HUNTING: A Primer of Strixine Intelligence

Snowy Owl

Nomadic creatures have to cope with the unexpected. They must make quick decisions—a lot of them. Often the data on which a critical life or death choice is based must be sensed, assimilated, and processed almost instantaneously. It is not an easy way of life. It requires stamina, flexibility, and a pretty fair share of plain old smarts.

An extraordinary example of on-the-spot problem solving was furnished a few years ago by a handsome male snowy owl. The place was Salisbury Beach, Massachusetts, at the mouth of the Merrimac River. A few days before the incident in question, a great Arctic rarity had shown up there—an ivory gull, a lovely boreal bird that seldom graces the lower

A snowy owl surveys the surrounding tundra from atop a small mound on a northern slope in Alaska.

latitudes. The presence of the gull brought crowds of eager birders from all over the Northeast to the parking lot of this otherwise bleak, unpeopled winter beach. A few duck hunters were also on the scene, and one of them shot a bufflehead, a pretty little bay duck, that fell down in the middle of a mud flat at low tide. Having no retriever to pick up his prize, the hunter left the duck lying on the mud. Suddenly the ivory gull, our honored guest from the frozen North, moved toward it. Hardly a moment later the visitor was challenged by a local resident, the greater black-backed gull. Black-backed gulls are big and mean. Ivory gulls, though pretty, are hardly cowards. In their native habitat they live together with walruses, not the most trustworthy of companions to have on an ice floe. So here we had a tough Arctic customer, used to dealing with walruses, facing down a Boston bully for the freshly killed duck. The gulls would back away from the duck and charge at each other. When they got within inches of each other's noses, they would stop, open their bills, hiss, and back off again. They did this four or five times.

In the meantime, not many feet away, a beautiful, pure white snowy owl watched the contest. It bided its time, and when the adversaries were separated at just the right distance, the owl made its move. With tremendous speed, it zoomed out of the marsh, snatched the bufflehead from the mud, flipped its body once, and flew away, glancing back at the two nonplussed gulls with what might have been pure contempt.

Barn Owl

As we have elsewhere noted, barn owls are among the most efficient mousers in the world. But their hunting prowess is not confined to taking mice, and they will readily adapt themselves to whatever food on the hoof or wing a particular environment provides. Consider the two following examples reported by A. C. Bent.

On an island off California Paul Bonnot found an abandoned cabin where barn owls were nesting underneath a wooden bedstead. The island was brimming with burrows of Leach's storm petrels. On these little Mother Carey's chickens the barn owls feasted, apparently exclusively. Bonnot found that the "area covered by the bed was three inches deep with feathers, wings, and bodies" of the hapless birds. The barnies had so little difficulty catching them that in many instances they simply bit off the heads, leaving the bodies perfectly intact.

In 1926, barn owls hunting in marshes in the vicinity of Charleston, South Carolina, were found to have eaten a large number of sora rails and clapper rails. Dr. Charles W. Townsend reported this find to Dr. A.A.K. Fisher, at that time the leading authority on avian nutrition. Fisher noted that rails "simulate the movements of rats and mice" and suggested that this imitative behavior might have caused their slaughter.

One of the most abundant songbirds of our prairie states is the dickcissel. A plump, sparrow-sized bird with a lemon yellow breast and a black gorget, it looks like a miniature meadowlark. Its main wintering grounds are the rice fields of Trinidad.

There the barn owls have mastered a special technique for catching them—strafing. The owls close their eyes and dive straight into the rice paddies, talons out, and go zooming through until they snag a morsel. This they do with amazing regularity. Between October and March the fields are so saturated with dickcissels that the owls need only worry about the arrival of April, when swelling gonads tell the prey that it is time once more to

A barn owl with captured mouse in beak, the usual method of carrying prey back to the nest. This owl is a very effective rat catcher and hunts in prime rodent territories.

fly north to Illinois. Then the owls have to go back to work for their food.

Any time the travel industry touts a new tropical paradise, we can say hello to a former tropical paradise. Several years back it was the turn of the Seychelle Islands. As long as the small native population of this Indian Ocean archipelago went its quiet way catching fish and carving coconuts, things went swimmingly for the local wildlife, including the colossal colonies of terns.

But by the time *Sports Illustrated* sent Christie Brinkley to decorate the islands and the cover of its bathing suit issue—along with George Plimpton to do a bit about the birds—the Seychelles' wildlife was already in retreat. A massive increase in tourism had begun to tear apart the fragile environmental webwork of the islands.

One of the first side effects of this ecological degradation was, not surprisingly, rats. These nasty camp followers of Western man swarmed over the Seychelles and began devouring the terns. Authorities wrung their hands in despair when someone suddenly remembered that barn owls were a safe and effective rodenticide. Eureka! Biological control! What could be better?

Barn owls were gleefully imported and released. For a while the solution really worked. The owls fell upon the rats and wiped them out. But when the rats were gone, there was nothing left for them to eat—except the terns, of course. And so the cure turned out to be itself a disease. Apparently, nobody had reckoned with the barnies' ability to take their food where they found it. Not only did the barnies gobble up the terns, but, being resourceful nesters, they took to excavating burrows in the sand in the thickest and most impenetrable parts of the palmetto scrub, making their eradication just about impossible. And there, thirty years later, things stand today. They could be a lot worse, though. The owl population has stabilized, being much less able to proliferate than rats, and the number of terns they take to maintain their numbers does not seem to threaten the tern colonies with annihilation, which the rats would almost certainly have brought about in the long run.

Screech Owl

Cooperative hunting has been observed in several raptor species. Ferruginous hawks use teamwork to take rabbits. Flocks of ravens are known to outwit wolves regularly. But to this writer's knowledge, cooperative hunting behavior among any of the nineteen species of North American owls has rarely been reported.

However, a few years ago, it was the privilege of the author to observe a group of screech owls take on a nest of robins in what was undeniably an example of cooperative hunting behavior.

In late summer screech owl families often stage what for lack of a better term might be called schmoozing sessions, the young often still doing the "branching" exercises typical of baby owls while the parent birds keep a lookout on the periphery of the roosting tree, often an old maple. Once in a while the parents will call to each other, almost always using a soft trill. The young meanwhile engage in vocabulary building sessions. For long periods they try out just about every sound their little voice boxes are capable of. One fledgling's long whinnies descend to the bottom of the scale, loop upward dramatically, and level off into a trill; the calling stops momentarily, then another fledgling takes up the refrain, followed by yet another. Then three soft trills fill the air simultaneously. Such vocal experimentation can go on for a good part of the night.

It was on a warm moonlit night that I listened to this particular screech owl family conducting a schmoozing session. Pleasantly occupied in taking notes on the owls' performances, I was suddenly surprised to hear the unmistakable alarm rattle of robins directly behind me.

There were at least four, possibly six, owls in the family. For at least two hours they had been moving back and forth along a stretch of a hundred feet or so of heavily wooded ridge across an abandoned dirt track in the Butler Preserve of the Nature Conservancy, in Mt. Kisco, New York. Behind me was a hemlock glen, and bordering the glen an open field with a brushy woodland border. Here the robins had their nest.

One or possibly two of the owls had flown across the dirt road into the hemlocks. They were whinnying loudly in the direction of the rattling robins. As the signaling went on, it was easy to see the shadow of another owl move rapidly across the open field to the right of the hemlock grove. The denouement was quick and dramatic. A plunge into a thicket, a tumult of agonized squeals and flying feathers, then utter silence. The terrain was such that approaching the scene of the kill to see the owls eat would have alerted them instantly and caused them to fly away. But I had no doubt of what I had witnessed: screech owls hunting cooperatively.

A spotted owl attacks a wood mouse.

NESTING:
A Primer of
Strixine
Domesticity

Even a casual scan of the literature reveals an inordinate amount of confusion—if not outright misinformation—regarding nest-building behavior among the owls.

Owls do not build nests. Some, like short-eared and snowy owls, produce simple scrapes, which they may or may not line with plant material. Burrowing owls, in a pinch, will dig their own burrows; barn owls have been known to do so, too. There is also evidence of some kind of vestigial nest-building ability in long-eared owls. It is so seldom utilized, however, as to be negligible.

owls and the specially designed boxes set out for screech and saw-whet owls to nest in.

The eggs of owls are pure white. They vary dramatically in both size and number. The eggs of an elf owl weigh seven grams; those of a great horned owl as much as sixty-five. Clutch size ranges from the two eggs of the typical horned owl nest to the six-to-seven-egg clutch of the short-eared owl. In situations of unusual prey abundance, extraordinarily large clutches have been reported for snowy owls (fourteen to fifteen), barn owls (eleven), and short-eared owls (sixteen).

Above: An elf owl fledgling perches in its nesting cavity in a saguaro cactus. The dense, moist saguaro allows the elf owl to remain cool while temperatures soar above 100° F just inches outside the cavity. Right: Two young great gray owlets sit in their nest.

What owls do for dwellings is to take over existing structures. Natural tree cavities suit the barred and spotted owls; at least ten species of small owls live in old woodpecker holes; great gray owls are attracted to mossy stumps; snowy owls love lichen-covered outcrops; great horned and long-eared owls use the abandoned nests of hawks, herons, squirrels, and crows; and several species nest on ledges or in crevices of cliffs. Finally, there are the manmade structures: the barns, abandoned buildings, and belfries haunted by barn

In every American owl species except the pygmy owls incubation begins when the first egg is laid. This gives rise to staggered or, as the experts like to call it, asynchronous hatching. In birds like the barn owl intervals of two to three days between eggs are normal. This means that in a large clutch of seven eggs, for example, by the time the last egg has pipped, the first owlet may already be two weeks old. Because of the rapid growth rate of the nestlings, this staggered hatching often serves as a kind of life insurance policy. The older fledg-

lings get the lion's share of what the parents catch. If one of the parents dies or if there is an unforeseen drop in prey availability, the older and better-fed siblings are likely to survive to adulthood and thus perpetuate the species.

Instances of siblicide—an older nestling devouring a smaller, weaker brother or sister—have been observed often enough to have created a large body of "Ruddigore" literature. There is no question that such things happen. Long ago, however, the author was struck by what he perceived were unusual circumstances surrounding many of these reports of strixine fratricide—in particular undue observer intrusion. In their magnificent monograph on the common barn owl Bunn, Warburton, and Wilson show that cannibalism among the young is a notably rare occurrence; moreover, siblings seldom steal food from each other, and older owlets will occasionally even try to feed their younger nest mates.

In most owl species incubation lasts about four weeks, with, of course, the expected variations: tiny elf owl babies may take only

Far left: Four young saw-whet owlets peer from their nesting cavity in the hollow of a dead tree stump. Above: A long-eared owl hatchling and two eggs in their nest, along with prey (a vole). Left: Snowy owl hatchlings.

twenty-one days to hatch; the massive off-spring of the great horned owl may take up to thirty-five.

As far as is known with certainty, only female owls brood, although there are unconfirmed reports of males assisting in the process in some species.

Males have their work cut out for them, though. Not only do they have to keep their mates in mice during the incubation period, but also after the owlets begin to hatch and the mother owls continue brooding the babies, sometimes for up to three weeks. It is then that the fathers must really hustle. They have to keep up their own vital signs, make sure the mothers' body heat doesn't go down, and provide enough chow for the children to grow. And let the reader recall that baby owls grow at a prodigious rate.

The brooding of babies is as endearing as it is intense. Few sights of nature are as affecting as a mother owl, like the great gray in Art Wolfe's study of domestic felicity, feeding a cluster of cuddly owlets clad in velvety down. As the owlets get bigger they often huddle close to the mother owl while she simply stands and spreads her wings over her brood.

The owlets rapidly build thick coats of down and reserves of body fat, so that eventually the mother is able to leave them and join her mate in hunting forays. This is quite providential in the case of great horned owls. At about three weeks of age the owlets have reached their full fledging weight. Their food intake requirements correspondingly peak. This coincides with increased prey availability as the warmer days of spring roll in. It also, mercifully for father owl, coincides with mama's ability to help him take in the increased provender and satisfy the voracious appetites of the brood.

Fledging patterns parallel the variations in egg size and hatching period length. Elf owls can fly in twenty-seven days, whereas great horneds may take up to seventy days before they become airborne.

When the young of small owl species first emerge to explore the big wide world, they are fully capable of flight. They exhibit a good deal of branching behavior—so delightfully captured in Wolfe's portrait of baby boreal owls—but they are quite capable of taking to the air in response, usually, to the urgings of the parents. At this stage of development saw-whet owls, boreal owls, and the several species of screech owls develop an extensive repertoire of behaviors related to the various types of expertise they must master to survive.

This training period, entailing the learning of complex visual and vocal signals, is no less marked in nestlings of species that breed in exposed places, such as the snowy, short-eared, long-eared, and great horned owls. In fact, it is more filled with incident, since a typical phase in the development of these owls consists of their abandoning the nest some-

times before half of the fledging period has elapsed. Typical is the great horned owl, whose young often spend from ten days to two weeks hopping about in branches and on the ground before they are fully capable of flight. Food is brought to them by their parents, who also guide the owlets in their experimental hunting as well as guard them against predators—or misguided human benefactors.

Left: Young boreal owlets perch in a display of branching behavior. Above: Five juvenile long-eared owls.

9

CONSERVATION

Left: A juvenile great gray owl perches on a tree stump after fledging the nest. Right: An adult burrowing owl concealed by reeds near its burrow entrance.

*P*eople shoot owls. Sometimes the shooting is for profit. Sometimes old superstitions well up and it is done out of fear. Typically, such atavistic behavior is rationalized: the mindless gunman explains that he killed the owl to save his chickens or his ducks or the local gamebirds. Yet, only one species, the great horned owl, has ever consistently been implicated in the loss of domestic fowl. And even with hornies, no instance of serious damage to poultry or gamebirds has ever occurred that did not involve negligence or an artificially induced imbalance, such as the release of pen-bred pheasants in the vicinity of nesting owls.

Shooting owls for lucre is another matter. Bounties for the slaughter of birds, thank heaven, are a thing of the past. Not so some men's incurable craving for stuffed carnivores to decorate their living rooms and dens. Tiger hunts are no longer practicable; ditto for lion safaris. But even if they were, a big cat would not look as comfortable on the mantel in a subdivision Tudor or ranch house as a plump snowy or great horned owl.

Today's owl hunter is too busy a man to put on a parka, go to the beach at Christmas time, and bag himself a snowy owl. Instead, he asks a taxidermist to get him one. The latter in turn pays a poacher, who goes out and shoots the owl. All of this, of course, is quite illegal. But it goes on. And don't believe that the increased popularity of bird-watching has reduced the incidence of poaching. On the contrary—the country teems with Rare Bird Alert hotlines (RBAs), and poachers have learned to use the telephone. They now dial for tips on where to find hot birds. Many RBAs no longer give directions to localities where a rare owl has been spotted. Some RBAs have stopped reporting rare raptors altogether. This is a great pity, but it is better than taking the chance of having the birds butchered.

Owls are also being poisoned.

A number of years ago, after long and bitter controversy, ecologists won a major battle against the use of DDT and other chlorinated hydrocarbons. The results have been spectacular. Ospreys, peregrine falcons, and bald eagles have more than just bounced back from the brink of extinction: they have staged a breathtaking comeback.

The downside of this has been a relaxation of the guard. Nothing can be more dangerous. Greedy chemical companies love nothing better than an uncritical, uninformed public. Their talent for cooking up, packaging, and peddling nostrums for every bug-induced ill, real or imaginary, besetting gardener or farmer is prodigious. In the Reagan years, with the screening function of regulatory agencies at an all-time low, this talent was given a virtually free rein. An avalanche of new and inadequately tested pesticides has been dumped on the market. Some have wound up killing a lot of animals that they were not supposed to harm. Among the most lethal of these chemicals is diazinon, a widely marketed bug-killer that, although banned for agricultural use in some areas, is being sold over the counter everywhere as of this writing.

DDT, dieldrin, and chlordane are still actively killing great horned owls in orchards and in residential areas where these three chemicals remain at levels potentially toxic to people as well as to owls. In this respect, the great horned owl is beginning to fulfill a grotesque new role: dying for the good of mankind. Regarded as one of the most effective indicators of terrestrial contamination, sick

hornies tell us when our own backyards are unsafe. Thus, if those that nest in your estate begin to kick the bucket, it's time to test your water and your homegrown veggies in the nearest poison control center before your zucchinis zap you. Can any irony be more bitter? Wildlife playing the part of the slaves who tasted the food of Roman emperors!

In the reckless production and proliferation

of pesticides in the 1950s entire ecosystems were contaminated. Responsively, a powerful grassroots conservation movement sprang up to check this madness, but its success in bringing about the banning of some chemical poisons and the cleaning up of chemical dump sites has been less than total. The pesticide makers, supported by agribusiness and abetted by mendacious politicians seeking to assure a steady flow of campaign funds, have seen to it that the work of environmental degradation continues, nevertheless. There is now a vast literature on the subject in both the scientific and the popular media. With respect to the pesticide poisoning of owls in particular, some of the best writing has been done by Ward Stone under the auspices of the New York State Department of Environmental

Adult snowy owl at nest with hatchlings.

A barred owl perches on a branch of an alder, searching for food.

Conservation; several of his publications are listed in the bibliography.

Shooting and poisoning have contributed in no small measure to the rise of raptor rehabilitation centers. One of these deserves special mention: the Owl Rehabilitation Research Foundation, in Vineland, Ontario. Much of the success of this outstanding institution is due to the special talents, dedication, and contagious enthusiasm of its founder, Katherine McKeever, one of the great champions of owl conservation.

The main objective of rehabilitation is to return a hawk or an owl to the wild. Sometimes this is not possible: a broken wing refuses to mend; an eye will not heal (depriving the owl of binocular vision, essential to hunting); a baby owl will become imprinted on its keepers and remain forever unable to accept others of its kind. Hawks and owls that cannot be released are used for educational purposes. They help the naturalist to dramatize the role raptors play in the economy of nature, as well as to focus attention on the intrinsic worth of these feathered hunters.

In these educational efforts the rehabilitator-naturalist inevitably comes to focus on the most pressing problem affecting birds of prey: loss of habitat.

The concept of the balance of nature presupposes enough nature for there to be a balance in. We've all heard horror stories about ecological disasters overseas. Often our response has been generous. Who can resist the plight of the mountain gorilla (and the martyrdom of Diane Fossey)? Or of the orangutan? And yet, though we have deplored the felling of rain forests in Brazil and Sumatra, the slash-and-burn farming in Central America, the pollution of Lake Baikal in the Soviet Union, we have failed fully to address the problem in our own backyards. There is hardly a residential site in America that does not abut or is not part of some form or another of habitat fragmentation that should never have taken place. Indeed, it continues unabated.

Perhaps because so much lip service is paid to conservation, so much complacent faith placed in zoning regulations, we have become desensitized to the slow attrition that is gradually but inexorably eroding away our natural patrimony. Most of us are masters at self-deception.

However, when the economic stakes of development are high enough there is little need for self-deception. The war is then less subtle, the politics more patently self-serving, if not unabashedly corrupt. The kind of conservation problem that arises is vividly exemplified by the case of the spotted owl, discussed below. There are also complex and subtle situations where conflicting interests, often genuine, overlap. Now and then, for instance, one must face the fact that the development of an ecologically important tract of upland pasture as a shopping mall or an airport may well be the only answer to pressing social and economic needs. The owl species most likely to be threatened by development of this kind is the short-eared owl.

No matter what the difficulties, habitat preservation remains the overwhelming priority in any meaningful strategy of wildlife preservation. The disappearance of hardwoods along river valleys has just about done in the ferruginous pygmy owl; shopping centers and the condo craze have squeezed short-eared owls out of critical hunting grounds; and the felling of conifers in the Northwest is slowly strangling the spotted owl, a bird at odds with nature as well as man.

To underscore a major area of owl conservation we can do no better than examine the plight of this peaceable, beleaguered, and singularly beautiful bird.

As has been noted elsewhere, some species of owls seem to be on the upswing. Some even give the impression of having gone on a prospecting binge. Every season birders find boreal, hawk, and great gray owls breeding in new areas, their total numbers also apparently increased. However, for every action there is a reaction. The range extensions and burgeoning populations of these species are counterbalanced by the shrinking range and dwindling numbers of others. In some instances a particular species shows signs of being displaced by an aggressive rival. This is particularly true of the spotted owl. Until recently barred owls and spotted owls were allopatric—they did not occupy the same range at nesting time. The barred owl was essentially an eastern sister species, albeit a more versatile and pugnacious one, of the spotted owl. Now the barred owls have muscled into spotty turf. And the spotties seem to be losing out.

There is little we can or should do to control this kind of natural phenomenon. But we certainly can and should try to give the spotted owls an even chance. Instead, we have allowed the agencies that oversee our state and federal forests to consent to the destruction by timber companies of immense tracts of Douglas fir and other coniferous softwoods, habitat of the spotty. And as more and more of our

majestic timberland winds up as chopsticks, paper pulp, or frames for Japanese screens, this rare, unique, and irreplaceable bird teeters precariously on the brink of the black hole that has already swallowed up the great auk, the Carolina parakeet, and the passenger pigeon—if indeed it has not already engulfed the Bachman's warbler, the Eskimo curlew, and the ivory-billed woodpecker.*

Vanishing habitat is also one of the difficulties of the short-eared owl. Environmentalists concerned with the well-being of this species face a tough challenge. With spotted owls the tradeoff is clear—the payoff of protecting the bird eclipses the sacrifices. With the short-eared owl things are not so simple. This bird requires extensive tracts of open country. Of many nesting sites destroyed or vacated in the last thirty years a whopping majority were close to coastlines, river valleys, or potentially arable land. This choice of real estate in a wild animal is fatal. It is also the choice of people, owl lovers included.

Detailed protocols for effective action on behalf of short-eared owls are beyond the scope of this overview. Nonetheless, a few guidelines can be suggested. First of all it is important to get a handle on some aspects of the bird's breeding ecology that have not been sufficiently recognized. For nesting to be consistently successful the short-eared owl seems to require (at least in northeastern suburban areas) some combination of marshland and adjacent upland pasture. It is likely that a similar situation may be operative in prairie habitat, where the birds commute from cattail marsh to peripheral grasslands. The marsh is where the nest is usually placed. The pastures or grasslands seem to be needed as hunting grounds to support a minimum viable number of nestlings.

Although an appreciation of the value to wildlife of tidal wetlands, marshes, bogs, and swamps has developed in the last twenty or so years, a similar conservation consciousness is lacking with respect to upland pastures. Countless hayfields, clearings, and medium-size truck farms, especially on the outskirts of cities, have succumbed to the automobile economy and peripheral urban expansion. Even small nonprofit suburban farms, many of them next to protected marshes, have repeatedly failed to get attention as places worthy of conservation.

Old loper, the short-eared, is supposed to nest in marshes. There are huge reaches of salt marsh along the shores of Long Island, and

---

* See also species account in Portfolio section.

the lopers used to love it there; now they have disappeared. Why? The answer is in land-use policies on the mainland. How much greenbelt space is dead-handed in Nassau and Suffolk counties? What percentage of it is grassland? Clearly not enough to meet the food requirements of the owls.

Lopers that once bred in Troy Meadows, New Jersey, probably abandoned that site for similar reasons. Much of the once-celebrated marsh is still there, but the perimeter is a jigsaw puzzle of asphalt and concrete. The famous little cluster of breeding short-eareds at Chappaquiddick, on the western end of Martha's Vineyard, is no longer there. The immediate and overwhelming impression that Chappaquiddick used to produce on the visitor was one of primeval tranquillity. Try making anyone there today believe it. The owls obviously measured the change and fled.

In short, despite the fact that many apparently suitable nesting areas have been preserved, the peripheral open country that the owls need to get enough food for themselves and their offspring is disappearing, converted into housing developments, industrial parks, and shopping malls at an ever-increasing rate. Can anything be done? In many cases probably not much. There is, however, an area in which a great deal can be done, both for short-eared owls and other animals, including ourselves—the preservation of agricultural lands. Our agricultural economy has made most small-to-medium farms unprofitable. Millions of acres of such farmland will inevitably be pounced on by developers unless counties and states devise effective tax relief strategies for farm owners, possibly under the aegis of greenbelt preservation programs.

Private land trusts, organizations such as the Nature Conservancy, town and county park departments, and state departments of conservation as well as departments of parks and recreation have a clear mandate to pool their talents in collective efforts to preserve and protect our rapidly dwindling open country. It isn't just pretty vistas of grass that are at stake. Rural America, with its barns and barnies, hangs in the balance. And with it, those extra field mice that will keep the many other species of owls happy.

Owls are creatures of rare beauty and unique biological interest. They play an enormously important role in the economy of nature. But even were they useless and dull, they are our fellow creatures, pursuing their lives with as important a purpose as we pursue ours, and for this reason alone they deserve our respect and protection.

A Northern spotted owl.

10

FINDING OWLS IN THE FIELD

Left: A saw-whet owl in a Douglas fir. Right: A ferruginous pygmy owl calls to its mate.

OUTDOORS WITH THE OWLS: A PRIMER FOR OWL PROWLERS

*C*ertain birds put birders on their mettle. Of these none are more challenging than owls. Not only are most of them nocturnal; many are also solitary and retiring. And when by sheer luck the birder happens to come across an owl in the open, the likelihood is that he will not see it at all because owls are virtuosos of concealment.

The most useful tool in an owler's kit is a knowledge of their calls. These are best learned by going into the woods with an experienced owler. Descriptions help fix a listening experience, but they rarely help to identify an unknown sound. Records and cassettes do help a little.* However, most of them provide only brief samples of typical vocalizations. With owl calls, as with love, there is no substitute for the real thing.

---

* See Discography for a list of commercially available recordings.

Fortunately, in owling the real thing is neither rare nor difficult to find. Owls are vocal creatures. And sauntering out into the woods on a fragrant, moonlit April night, in quest of the wonders of the night world, is one of the most sensuous activities available to the student of nature. Even a winter owl prowl has its special appeal. The tremolos of screech owls floating across a frozen marsh, a great horned owl asserting his feudal rights over a pine-clad hillside, the pitch-black contours of land forms etched against an ultramarine sky—it is an experience worth the best parka money can buy.

A few hints for the prospective owl prowler.

With some exceptions, most of our woodland owls call at dawn and dusk. The best times for an owl prowl, therefore, are the two or so hours just after sunset and the two or three hours just before sunrise.

There are also more or less likely environs in which the birds can be found: a swamp-bordered wooded hillside in the Northeast for barred, screech, and great horned owls; a muskeg in Ontario for long-eareds, saw-whets, and a possible boreal owl; a pine-clad ravine in Oregon for spotted and flammulated owls; a mid-altitude clearing in Madera Canyon, Arizona, for just about anything. The first thing to do is defuse your nine-to-five circuitry; become part of the humus; meditate yourself into a tree stump. In other words, be quiet and take in nature's vibes. If an owl calls and you can talk back to it, by all means do so. Many owl calls are easily imitated. Chances are it's a territorial bird announcing its rights. You might sound like a mate or perhaps like a rival—in either case the landlord will very likely fly out to inspect you. This can be quaint if the owl is a saw-whet or disquieting if it happens to be a great horned, but it is always thrilling.

If no owl calls are heard and you know which owls are likely to be present in your chosen site, you may try to get the ball rolling by calling out first, using your voice or the great whistle you first developed for cheering at ballgames. If you neither hoot nor whistle, take along a tapedeck with a tape of prerecorded owl calls. After thousands of hours of owl prowling over the last twenty years, I am convinced it doesn't make the slightest bit of difference whether you start with a pygmy or a spotted, a great horned or a screech owl call. Traditional protocols emphasize the pecking order of cannibalism among owls—great horneds eat barred owls; barreds eat long-eareds; long-eareds eat screech owls; screech owls don't regularly eat saw-whets but do beat the daylights out of them. Therefore, the standard advice goes, do a great horned hoot and you will terrify every other owl in the neighborhood; play the barred and all the long-eared owls will cringe—and so on down the line. In other words, at each stop you should start with the tiniest owl and work gradually upward to the biggest.

For years I faithfully followed this code until the owls taught me differently. Screech owls readily and vigorously mob great horned and long-eared owls. On a grueling, bitter February census of possible great horned owl nests I made ten stops in what I thought were choice chunks of *Bubo* habitat. I hooted most convincingly—and pulled out ten very angry screech owls. In a hemlock ravine bordering the Hudson River at dusk in late November, a huge female great horned owl flew directly at me in response to my imitation of a male's mating call; at the same time a pair of long-eared owls, yapping like Pomeranians, flew up the canyon and drove my new girlfriend away. During an early fall census of screech owls I had tallied a grand total of twenty-four individuals in six separate groups, when three long-eared owls—later ascertained to be a family group—began calling and flying about. Nothing could have surprised me more than the reaction of the screech owls. Seven of them began flying in tight circles around the bigger long-eared owls, landing, flying again, and constantly calling. Surprisingly, many of the calls were of the long trill variety, generally associated with pair formation and nest defense. And as for saw-whets, I have seen them repeatedly stare down death by valiantly sallying forth against screech owls.

With regard to calling owls in pecking order, I am reminded of an incident. Some years ago a splendid wooded glen was going begging in the Christmas Bird Count. A friend of mine finally agreed to take it on and in the process check it out at night for owls. Prior to the occasion, I had given him a tape of saw-whet owl calls. What prompted him to play it I'll never know, since saw-whets hardly ever call in winter. But play it he did. Not far from my friend, as it happened, a great horned owl was sitting, waiting for supper. My tape was the menu: saw-whet owl au jus! *Bubo* sailed out and dove at my friend full-tilt, no doubt expecting him to produce a nice doe-eyed little owl. Friend ducked, *Bubo* swooshed by, and a great horned owl was added to his count.

Thus, the word to owl prowlers is this: go from small to big if you feel like it, but be forewarned that you may get your head knocked off in the process.

Squeak and Ye Shall Find

Here are a few more hints on pulling owls out of the bush. Hisses and squeals often work wonders. Many owls react strongly to snakes. Their ears are finely attuned to distress signals. The forlorn squeal of a lost cottontail, the cheeps of frightened field mice, the hissing of a cornered garter snake—all of these are powerful attractants. Any owl hearing a noise that suggests such anxiety in a prey animal is likely to believe that an easy meal is nearby and will act accordingly.

Trolling Owls

Riddle: What is the owl's favorite dessert? Answer: Chocowlate Mouse. Application: Take a mouse-shaped piece of wood, cover it with brown felt, tie it to the monofilament on your spinning rod, and go fishing—for owls.

Many owl investigators have used this elementary trick to lure strix out of the bush for the purpose of banding and color-coding. But it can also be useful in field birding—for example, in pulling a reluctant saw-whet owl out of a thicket. Saw-whets, like many other owls, just can't resist a moving target. They are drawn to such a lure like iron shavings to a magnet. The technique has drawbacks, of course. Surf casting in the woods can be tricky. Still, a small rod and reel kit can be toted about in a case and assembled on the spot.

Obviously, such a kit is optional equipment. The basic equipment for owling comprises a good tape player, a decent pair of binoculars, and a strong flashlight or lantern, preferably one with a built-in arc light powered by a long-lasting alkaline battery. But the prospective owl prowler must be warned never to use artificial illumination except when it is absolutely necessary. If used indiscriminately, it can completely wreck your night vision. It should only be turned on when there is a decent chance of being able to focus the beam on a nice-looking owl.

To all these hints on how to find owls a cautionary note must be added. Time was when birding was an elitist pastime. Under the aegis of the great Ludlow Griscom, father of field identification, bird-watching and Boston Brahminism were virtually synonymous. Long ago, however, the field glass fraternity mercifully ceased to be within the exclusive purview of patricians. Unfortunately, the popularity of the sport spawned a new phenomenon, "The Ugly Birder"—so named by Frank Graham in an article published by *Audubon* magazine several years ago.

One of the most flagrant abuses perpetrated by these Rambolike listers is the indiscriminate use of tape-recorded territorial songs. As all birders know by now, these songs are powerful attractants. A territorial male hearing the song of another male of the same species will interpret it as a challenge and fly out to do battle.

Corkscrew Swamp is the barred owl capital of southern Florida. A while back the Rambos blitzed the place so relentlessly with barred owl calls that they brought the breeding cycle of the birds to a complete halt. Not one single pair of barred owls in the entire sanctuary succeeded in rearing young. The managers finally had to confiscate tape recorders at the entrance.

In Arizona, the nesting cycle of elegant trogons has repeatedly been disrupted in the same way, probably by the same people who pull spotted owls away from their domestic duties by provoking them to attack electronic intruders. As previously noted, spotted owls are rare and endangered.

Birds have also been injured by the Rambos' heavy weapons. In 1988 a boreal owl died in Toronto. It perished from starvation because it could not hunt. Its eyes had been burned out by photographers' flashguns.

An animal cannot protest or defend itself against such sophisticated cruelty. We birders must act responsibly and responsively. The keynote is caution. If there is any suspicion in your mind that your owl-finding strategies have a detrimental effect, *don't use them*. Owls are in trouble enough from habitat destruction, pesticide poisoning, and illegal hunting. It would be tragic if their admirers were to add to these miseries.

11

WHERE TO FIND THE BIRDS
A "Travowlogue"

Left: An adult male snowy owl. Right: An elf owl fledgling perches on a prickly pear cactus blossom.

Many regional guidebooks provide exhaustive coverage of birding localities. In addition, the reader should consult the magnificent A Guide to Bird Finding *(in two volumes: East and West of the Mississippi) by Olin Sewall Pettingill, Jr. What is presented here are descriptions of major areas where owls as well as other natural wonders may be found without risking life and limb. A north to south, west to east format is as good as any, so let's begin, as the ballad says, "Way up yonder in the frozen north."*

THE HIGH ARCTIC/ALASKA

Hardy souls inspired by *Nanook of the North* may want to look for nesting snowy owls in such spots as **Point Barrow** or **Nome**, Alaska. This entails stamina, native guides, and more than a little cash. But the rewards can be extraordinary. In addition to owls, the birder willing to spend money and time—and battle mosquitoes—will enjoy unforgettable views of musk oxen, caribou, polar bears, and other arctic specialties.

A more conventional Alaskan owl prowl might begin in Anchorage, starting point for trips to **Mount McKinley National Park.** The park offers unexcelled opportunities for viewing a wide gamut of Alaskan wildlife, including hawk and boreal owls, but the possibilities vary with site and season. The visitor should consult the knowledgeable wardens at park headquarters as to these.

THE CANADIAN ROCKIES

As the owl finder moves south two Canadian national parks claim his attention: **Banff** and **Jasper.** These magnificent preserves are worth visiting on almost every imaginable count. As to the owls, this author is reminded of a talk given by an owl expert in Vancouver at a conference on birds of prey. As nonchalantly as if he were reporting the results of a chickadee census, the speaker told a crowd of open-mouthed listeners that in five or six seasons in Banff and Jasper he had succeeded in banding 1,500 individual boreal owls. The author does not recall the number of great gray owls that he also claimed to have captured, but it, too, was mind-boggling. The parks offer topflight possibilities for finding these and several other owl species. In addition, of course, the visitor can expect to see a rich variety of montane wildlife. Details about the parks and the many attractions in their periphery may be obtained from the Canadian Tourist Bureau.

THE PACIFIC NORTHWEST

Washington

South of British Columbia one comes to an area of special interest. For exceptional owl finding in settings of unparalleled natural beauty few regions in the United States rival and none surpasses the **Northern Cascades, Mount Rainier,** and **Olympic Peninsula.** Indeed, it is in this area of unique panoramic splendor that Art Wolfe has taken many of the fabulous photographs in this book.

One of Wolfe's favorites is the pygmy owl. No setting for enjoying these delightful birds is finer than the fairyland of **Olympic National Park.** And it is hard to conceive of a more enchanting place to look for such elusive specialties as the spotted owl than **Mount Rainier National Park.** A word of warning to the owl seeker who chooses Mount Rainier to hoot out his first spotted owl: you may never come back. The place has a Shangri-la quality that can bewitch you.

It may perhaps be superfluous to say this, but the nature study possibilities that present themselves to anyone visiting Mount Rainier, the Cascades, and Olympic Peninsula are almost endless. What is particularly nice about falling under the spell of the Northwest is the fact that one can proceed south along Route 101 all the way to the Big Sur in California with hardly a break in the dream. Yes, the Northwest does have its timber barons, and Mother Nature did blow a monstrous aneurysm on the flank of Mount St. Helens. But the southbound owl seeker will quickly regain the magic in Oregon.

Oregon

Oregon offers another constellation of natural wonders in which the lesser stars are great and the major ones are almost indescribable. An area the owler will find especially rewarding is **Mount Hood** and the adjacent **Hood River Valley.** Like Rainier, Hood is an active volcano, towering above the surrounding Cascade Mountains. And as in Rainier, one can begin birding above tree line. Going down the mountain, the birder may enjoy the unfolding spectacle of layered life zones, each with its characteristic flora and fauna. Owling in the various habitats of Hood, as well as the wooded valleys at its base, should yield a big list of local species.

South and west of Mount Hood is Mount Mazama, a volcano that blew its top aeons ago, creating what many believe to be the loveliest lake in the world. This is **Crater Lake National Park.** In 1956 Roger Tory Peterson and the great British ornithologist James Fisher visited the park and were so dazzled by its beauty that they had to pretend it was unreal in order to get through the day. Owl finding was probably not on their schedule—

not many come to Crater Lake with *Strix* or *Bubo* in mind—but the owls are there: great horned owls, screech owls, pygmies, long-eared, and spotted owls—owls *ad libitum*. In fact, the problem with the park, as with so many wild areas of the West, is getting *away* from wildlife. In Crater Lake the birds come at you. You can't miss with Mount Mazama.

En route to redwood country the owler may want to take a gander at the throngs of waterfowl in **Lake Malheur** and the **Klamath Basin.** As of the 1980s, a dense conifer forest just south of the town of **Fort Klamath** has had a sizable resident population of great gray owls. On the California border, the **Siskiyou Mountains** offer good possibilities for owl prowls.

CALIFORNIA

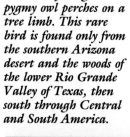

An adult ferruginous pygmy owl perches on a tree limb. This rare bird is found only from the southern Arizona desert and the woods of the lower Rio Grande Valley of Texas, then south through Central and South America.

California is a cornucopia of wonders. Its coast alone is 1,200 miles long. It has the tallest trees in the world, the highest peak in the U.S. south of Canada, the lowest desert on the continent, and until recently one of the largest flying birds in the world—the California condor. Owl finding in California is predictably superlative.

San Francisco is ideal as a base for a variety of excursions. One of these should be to the coastal redwoods. **Redwood National Park** is the classic spot for taking in these giant trees and their specialized birdlife, including the rare spotted owl.

Another excursion should take the owl finder to **Yosemite National Park.** This magnificent preserve features all the avian associations of the Sierra Nevada. For years it was the locality of choice for great gray owls in the

U.S. Though harder to find today (possibly because of observer pressure), this owl species is still a Yosemite specialty. So is the pygmy owl, which can be heard and seen in conjunction with its late-night replacement species, the saw-whet owl.

High on the western flank of the Sierra Nevada, in central California, are **Sequoia** and **Kings Canyon national parks.** Together they comprise 1,324 square miles of magnificent forest that not only includes the giant sequoias, but ponderosa pines, cedars, firs, willows, aspens, dogwoods, and oaks. The birdlife is as rich as that in Yosemite and the owl finding no less so.

Birders who come to **Monterey** for the famous whale and seabird-watching trips or to see the rookeries at Point Lobos should not miss the chance to whistle out the owls here:

A screech owl in a salmonberry bush.

pygmies from the Monterey pines, western screech owls from the pine-oak stands, and saw-whets from the nearby Big Sur woodlands.

At one time or another almost everyone who travels to California winds up in Los Angeles. The city elicits strong reactions: some hate it, some love it; but one thing everyone must agree on—it's a fantastic place for nature study. From Los Angeles one can take off in a dozen different directions, exploring natural areas of bewildering variety. Most notable for bird-life—including woodland owls—and readily accessible are the **San Gabriel Mountains.**

Other natural areas—not necessarily first-rate for owl finding on an individual basis, but cumulatively well worthwhile—are the **San Bernardino Mountains,** the **Salton Sea Basin,** the **Mojave** and **Colorado deserts, Joshua Tree National Monument,** and last but emphatically not least, **Death Valley National Monument.**

For many the temptation to visit Death Valley is irresistible. If you yield you will not be sorry. Of course, most people don't come here for owls. The place is a showcase of history and geology. But you will be pleasantly surprised to discover that burrowing owls breed on the slopes at mid-altitude (April is the best month to find them) and that great horned owls frequent the cliffs, where one may also enjoy excellent views of prairie falcons, one of our most dashing diurnal birds of prey.

THE CONTINENTAL DIVIDE NORTH

Idaho

There is no better way to take in Idaho's wilderness in all its kaleidoscopic variety than to drive U.S. 93 from **Salmon** to **Hailey** (or vice versa). This two-hundred-mile stretch will take you from cloud-cleaving summits to deep valleys, across canyons and forests, and offer views of many mountain-girded lakes. The full spectrum of high country birds may be found by stopping and exploring suitable habitats. At least nine species of owls can be encountered in this way, including boreals and great grays.

Boise is the starting point for a visit to the **Snake River Birds of Prey Natural Area.** From early March to mid-June this thirty-three-mile stretch of the Snake River Canyon offers magnificent views of golden eagles and up to eight species of hawks and falcons. At least seven species of owls are known to occur in this unique wildlife preserve.

Montana

Glacier National Park is monumental. For scenic impact it rivals Banff and Jasper. Lofty peaks, precipitous cliffs, cloud-girded glaciers, valleys framed by razorback ridges, hundreds of meltwater lakes, and a profusion of streams and waterfalls all blend in a landscape of alpine magnificence. The park is a backpacker's paradise. Most of its primeval wilderness is accessible only by trails, over 1,000 miles of them. Though some fine areas, including woods where owls nest, may be reached by car, Glacier is a place where long-distance trekking really pays off: the rewards make the blisters worthwhile.

Wyoming

More superlatives have been lavished on **Yellowstone National Park** than any other spot in the nation. If you breathe, you've heard about the wonders of this park, unquestionably the greatest natural showcase in North America. Ironically, most descriptions do not give a true picture of the place. When you go there—and you certainly should—you will probably be startled at how different the park is from what you thought it would be.

This has nothing to do with the great fires of 1988. Yellowstone is a rich and varied amalgam of habitats with a correspondingly rich and varied fauna. The fires did not destroy all of this natural wealth. Though the populations of certain forest-dwelling species probably declined, the park is still a premier spot for birds of prey, including the lordly great gray owl.

South of Yellowstone in western Wyoming is **Grand Teton National Park.** The park and its satellites, **Jackson Hole, National Elk Refuge,** and **Rendezvous Mountain,** are as outstanding a constellation as any wild America has to offer. Here the Craighead brothers, Frank and John, did pioneer research on hawks and owls forty years ago. Frank Craighead updated this work in 1981. When raptor mavens of this caliber pick out a research area you better believe it's good.

Here a birder may bask in the bliss of sighting bald eagles and great gray owls side by side with ospreys and golden eagles; red-tailed hawks and great horned owls; pygmy owls, sharp-shinned hawks, Cooper's hawks, and northern goshawks; short-eared owls and northern harriers; Swainson's hawks, long-eared owls, prairie falcons, kestrels . . . the list goes on. At least fourteen species of raptors, together with incredible assemblages of marsh birds, waterfowl, and songbirds, may be observed here in settings of ineffable scenic grandeur.

THE CENTRAL ROCKIES

Nevada

Las Vegas—yes, *the* Las Vegas of Caesar's Palace, one-armed bandits, and night owls of a different kind is a good departure point for first-rate bird finding in a diverse array of habitats. The best owl localities will probably be in the **Charleston Mountains.** Other Nevada sites with good owling potential are the **Toiyabe Mountains** (reached from Austin) and the bottomlands and desert washes of **Lake Mead National Recreation Area** (reached from Boulder City).

Utah

For great horned owls few places are as productive as the pinyon-juniper woodlands of central Utah. Most birders who visit the state are attracted to Brigham City, for the **Bear River Migratory Bird Refuge,** one of the finest in the country, and to **Salt Lake City,** for the Seagull Monument and the many natural attractions in its environs. Details on owl finding can readily be obtained at Bear River

Refuge headquarters, as well as from the **Utah Audubon Society** in Salt Lake City. Another source of ornithological information is the **M. L. Bean Life Science Museum** at Brigham Young University in Provo. The latter city also offers easy access to the best habitats in the **Wasatch Range,** including spectacular Mount Timpanogos.

Colorado

Colorado is high country: 1,500 peaks reach 10,000 feet or more; 300 top 13,000 feet; 52 tower above 14,000 feet. This is great for skiers and boreal birds, including the boreal owl. Probably here since nature made it, this species with the voice of a musical snipe has only recently been found to nest in Colorado. Another specialty, the flammulated owl, may be sighted in spruce woods and aspen parklands.

Good localities for finding forest birds may be reached from Boulder (**Mount Audubon**) and Colorado Springs (**Black Forest**). But for the best of the Colorado Rockies, **Denver**

A great gray owl atop the stump of a Douglas fir.

can't be beat. Several areas, known as the **Mountain Parks,** offer unexcelled opportunities for finding birds of the high country, including a possible boreal owl. Of many possible trips from Denver, the one to **Mount Evans** may be combined with visits to three mountain parks: **Red Rocks Park, Genesee Park,** and **Echo Lake Park.**

THE SOUTHWEST

Arizona

Arizona is the Eden of strixine addicts. Blessed with a unique mix of habitats, the state has a correspondingly unusual fauna. The owls are a well-known component of this rich wildlife.

In a picturesque mountain setting, **Flagstaff** boasts several topflight bird-finding spots, none better than **Oak Creek Canyon,** which is in fact an ecological wonderland. The night birder in Oak Creek should be especially alert for the calls of spotted and flammulated owls.

Arizona's premier tourist attraction is **Grand Canyon National Park.** It's huge and the hucksters have hyped it too much, but you can take it in bit by bit and let its grandeur burn off the bad vibes. A first-rate spot for flammulated owls is the South Rim, close to park headquarters. It's hard to imagine finding a rare owl more conveniently, or with a more breathtaking backdrop.

Tucson is the traditional point of departure for pilgrimages to the bird meccas of southern

Arizona. These include portions of three mountain ranges, the **Huachucas,** the **Chiricahuas,** and the **Santa Ritas.** Some places are absolute musts. One is the **Arizona-Sonora Desert Museum,** a class act if ever there was one. Here a visitor may get a first taste of desert wildlife, buy books about the area—no less than five major references to Arizona birdlife are in print—and pick up information as to what the owls might be up to in **Madera Canyon** (gateway to the Santa Ritas) and **Cave Creek Canyon** (gateway to the Chiricahuas).

A typical Arizona big night begins in broad daylight with a scan of ranch country for burrowing owls. The next stop will be in the lower foothills for elf and ferruginous pygmy owls. Going up one of the canyons, the owler will find in ascending levels the home turf of western screech, northern pygmy, whiskered, flammulated, and finally saw-whet owls in the high country. En route, with any luck, he will have picked up great horned, long-eared, and spotted owls. Home at night's end, he might cap off this superprowl back at the ranch, with a barn owl doing its predawn duty of ridding the world of mice.

New Mexico

New Mexico is famous for the beauty and diversity of its natural habitats. The life-zone layer-cake topography typical of Arizona canyons is found in many mountainous areas of this state. The faunal variety in such places is also great. In some localities an owl tally of up to eight species is possible.

Of the many mountain ranges, the most tempting are the northern extensions of Mexico's **Sierra Madre.** These are best reached from Lordsburg, on the Mexican border. This city offers convenient access to the **Peloncillo Mountains** and the **Lower Gila River Valley.** Burrowing owls are a specialty in the latter locality.

Lordsburg is also the point of departure for an exciting trip to **Guadalupe Canyon.** This remote and thoroughly wild place (also reachable from Douglas, Arizona) has a romantic reputation for rattlesnakes, bandits, and buff-collared nightjars, a rare relative of the whip-poorwill. The many birds of prey, including

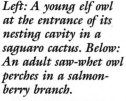

Left: A young elf owl at the entrance of its nesting cavity in a saguaro cactus. Below: An adult saw-whet owl perches in a salmonberry branch.

owls—not to mention a fine array of Mexican border wildlife—make the temptation to explore the place irresistible.

No place in New Mexico offers nicer possibilities for trips to wild country than Silver City. **Cherry Creek Canyon** and the **Gila River Valley** are only two of the many outstanding nearby natural areas.

Owl species to be looked for in the Lordsburg and Silver City areas include barn, great horned, flammulated, western screech, whiskered, pygmy, elf, burrowing, and spotted. Long-eared, short-eared, and saw-whet owls also occur within the state.

Texas

Superlative in all respects, **Big Bend National Park** is a must in any naturalist's Texas itinerary. Encompassing the Chisos Mountains, the park features terrain as wild and rugged as any in North America. Barn, western screech, great horned, and burrowing owls may be observed in this setting of primeval grandeur. The south-central Texas race of the barred owl breeds close to Big Bend and may occur within park boundaries. In winter the long-eared owl regularly swells the ranks of resident species.

Harlingen is the spot at which to take bearings for exploring the **Lower Rio Grande Valley.** This is one of the few areas in the U.S. where ferruginous pygmy owls could still occasionally be found in the 1980s.

The **Santa Ana National Wildlife Refuge** and nearby **Bentsen–Rio Grande Valley State Park** feature a wide gamut of Mexican border specialties. Elf owls and screech owls are definite nightbird possibilities, as are three species of nightjars, including the pauraque, a local specialty. Another local specialty, the plain chachalaca, is a gloriously noisy chicken-like bird. Owlers will find mid-April best for prowling here.

Other notable natural areas close to Harlingen are the **Laguna Atascosa National Wildlife Refuge** and **Falcon Dam.**

THE NORTHERN PRAIRIES

North Dakota

Best known for the Badlands, North Dakota also harbors huge throngs of grebes, ducks, geese, rails, sandpipers, and other water and marsh birds. Along with these, several national wildlife refuges (NWRs) offer unexcelled views of courting short-eared owls—the champion aerialists of the tribe. Their maneuvers may be enjoyed along with those of tremendous assemblages of avocets, gulls, and terns. The prairie grasslands offer burrowing owls, frequently side by side with marbled godwits, a shore bird second only to the avocet in size and beauty.

The best of the national wildlife refuges are **Des Lacs NWR, Lostwood NWR,** and the **J. Clark Salyer NWR.** *Note:* An extraordinary natural event to be enjoyed along with the roller-coastering of short-eared owls is the spectacular aquatic ballet of mating western grebes.

South Dakota

People who assume that the **Black Hills** are a spinoff of the Rockies, put in South Dakota just so Mount Rushmore could be carved to slow down traffic, make a big mistake. The area is unique and exciting in too many ways to be detailed here. A beautiful description of Black Hills birdlife may be found in Pettingill's classic guide. His seven-page paean to this natural wonderland makes it clear why no area in the country presents better chances for finding owls—along with just about every other bird in the book.

Minnesota

To anyone with even a casual interest in owls Minnesota is a mythic place. The first confirmed nest of boreal owls in the U.S. was found here. In the late 1980s hawk owls also bred in the state. Great gray owls have also nested in Minnesota.

Two different strategies are suggested for the owl finder. The first is a visit to the **Hawk Ridge Nature Preserve** and the north shore of **Lake Superior,** both close to Duluth, during the fall hawk flights. Here, especially in October when the hawks close up shop for the day, migrant owls take over, the most abundant being the delightful saw-whet owl.

The second is a trip to **Quetico-Superior Canoe Area,** an immense natural area on both

Left: A flammulated owl peers out from its nest cavity within a mature aspen tree. Above: A burrowing owl on a dead shrub near the entrance to its burrow.

sides of the U.S.-Canada border that has been set aside as wilderness in perpetuity by international agreement. This is a paddler's paradise. On the American side, portions of **Superior National Forest** may be reached by car. But Quetico-Superior will yield its finest treasures to the adventurous canoeist. The facilities will be the ones you take with you. Take them, and take the plunge.

For those who may find such a strenuous trip impossible, a visit to the **Red Lake Wildlife Management Area,** close to Baudette, is recommended. Comprising almost half a million acres, the area is a showcase for many species of raptors. These include all the Minnesota owl specialties, as well as seven nesting species of hawks and falcons.

THE CENTRAL PRAIRIES

Nebraska

One of the greatest natural spectacles in North America takes place each year from March 15 to April 15 along the **Platte** and **North Platte rivers** in Nebraska. Thousands of sandhill cranes and a handful of whooping cranes loiter on the mudflats, fatten up in the cornfields, and begin pair formation by performing a series of bizarre leaping dances. This rite of passage attracts almost as many birders as cranes.

If you come to see the cranes you should not miss the local burrowing owls. The immediate vicinity offers unparalleled opportunities for enjoying them at the height of their antics. To round out a unique trio of specialties, you can also see and hear the dawn dances of the greater prairie chicken at this time. Dancing cranes, booming prairie chickens, and bowing billy owls: no reservations needed for Nebraska's "Rite of Spring."

THE MIDWEST

Illinois

Close to the great metropolis of Chicago, 65,000 acres of diverse natural areas are managed by the **Forest Preserve District of Cook County.** Among the many sanctuaries, nature centers, and reservations controlled by the

Forest Preserve District, the **Palos Park Forest Preserve,** comprising 10,000 acres of hardwood forest, is probably the best owl-finding spot. Just south of the Forest Preserve is the **McGinnis Slough Wildlife Refuge,** famous for waterfowl, waders, and marsh birds, but also good for owls in the forested higher terrain.

In southern Illinois a natural area of great scenic beauty is **Père Marquette State Park,** easily reached from Grafton and quite close to St. Louis, Missouri. Located at the confluence of the Illinois and Mississippi rivers, the park is richly forested and has very varied terrain. The list of resident birds is predictably impressive. Night birders can confidently expect to find all the local species of owls and nightjars.

Michigan

Close to Detroit, though strictly speaking not in Michigan but over the border in Canada, is **Point Pelee National Park.** This extraordinary mecca for May migrants, feathered and unfeathered, lures almost everyone with even a moderate interest in birds at one time or another. Owl finding at Pelee can be rewarding but is usually neglected in favor of more spectacular sights. If owls are your quarry,

check out possibilities at park headquarters.

Isle Royale National Park, a magnificent roadless wilderness, is not for the ordinary tourist. You will have to find your nesting hawk owls, saw-whets, and possible boreals or great grays on foot. Celebrated for its packs of wild wolves (they prey on equally wild herds of moose), this is a place for true wilderness trekking. Surrounded by two hundred outlying islands and islets, this 210-square-mile island park is thirteen miles from the nearest mainland.

Few places in the U.S. offer the nature lover such remarkable expanses of varied and unspoiled wilderness as Michigan's north country. And few areas afford so many chances for studying the northern forest owls. An excellent base of operations for forays in the Upper Peninsula is Newberry. Of several sites in the vicinity, the most outstanding is the area around **Sleeper Lake** and the **Seney National Wildlife Refuge.**

THE APPALACHIANS

Pennsylvania

Few bird sanctuaries ever become a major tourist attraction. That distinction surely belongs to **Hawk Mountain Sanctuary** in the environs of Drehersville. No place in Pennsylvania pulls in the crowds as surely as this unique preserve, dedicated to the high art and contagious lunacy of looking at migrating hawks. Hawk flights peak from mid-September through October. By late November most of the hawks have fled the cold and joined the yuppies in Acapulco. Not so the owls. Many of them are permanent residents, and members of the sanctuary staff study them assiduously. A check at sanctuary headquarters will give you the current status of owl study projects there.

Kentucky

People come to Cave City for **Mammoth Cave National Park.** There are three reasons for going there: the caves are mind-boggling; no better place exists for studying the wood warblers—sixteen species breed in the park; and it has primitive, heavily wooded areas where the nightbird finder will be treated to a magnificent if eerie chorus of eastern screech owls, great horned owls, and barred owls joining forces with the two eastern forest nightjars, the whippoorwill and the chuck-will's-widow, to fill the night air with whinnies, wails, boomings, and incessant name calling by the "whips" and "chucks."

THE SOUTHERN APPALACHIANS

The topographic and ecological amplitude of the southern Appalachians beggars description. Here we can detail just a few famous spots. Many others can be found described in Maurice Brooks's informative and delightful *The Appalachians.*

West Virginia

Below Canaan Mountain are the 25,000 acres of **Canaan Valley.** Featuring sphagnum bogs and densely timbered slopes, it has long been noted for productive bird finding. Close to Elkins, the **Cheat Mountains** are of great in-

terest to naturalists, and **Gaudineer Knob,** in the Cheat Range, is a well-known bird study area. The **Cranberry Glades,** near Marlinton, are a subalpine remnant of the glacial era, holding faunal and floral elements characteristic of boreal ecosystems. Studying the birdlife of these localities, including owls, has always been exceptionally rewarding.

Virginia

Shenandoah National Park, in the heart of the Blue Ridge Mountains, is as beautiful a place as a birder can take in and still keep

An adult great gray owl perches on a Douglas fir branch.

enough of his cool to tally up a decent list. A scenic journey down the 105-mile **Skyline Drive** can make finding owls (and anything else) in the Blue Ridge sheer bliss.

Just shy of the North Carolina border, **Mount Rogers** (5,719 ft.), highest peak in Virginia, and **White Top Mountain** are of particular interest to the owl finder. A road to the summit of White Top makes it possible to go from barred owl habitat at the bottom to saw-whet turf at the top.

North Carolina

In North Carolina the Skyline Drive becomes the **Blue Ridge Parkway.** The owler's first stop should be lofty **Mount Mitchell** (6,684 ft.), highest peak on the eastern seaboard and a premier locality for saw-whet owls. The next area, **Craggy Gardens,** offers views of rhododendron "balds." In June these dense growths form spectacular carpets of flowers close to the summits. **Mount Pisgah,** tops for tourist amenities, is notable for ecological diversity. Southwest of Pisgah the parkway winds its way through high altitude forests of spruce and fir, with overlooks and nature trails that offer opportunities for finding high country birds, especially saw-whet owls. **Devil's**

Courthouse, Tanasee Bald, and **Richland Balsam** are recommended stops.

Tennessee

The Blue Ridge Parkway ends at the Tennessee border, bringing the traveler to forests of incomparable magnificence and the **Great Smoky Mountains National Park,** one of the few genuinely unique ecological wonderlands on the continent. For density of temperate deciduous trees the park's forests—half of them virgin timber—are unrivaled anywhere on earth, except possibly by a few montane tracts in China.

Predictably, the fauna of these mountains is varied and rich. Other than the often mentioned saw-whet owls, always found at the highest altitudes, the Smokies offer suitable habitats for eastern screech owls, great horned owls, barred owls, and long-eared owls and harbor the hawks that are their diurnal replacement species.

Not to be missed is the drive to the summit of **Clingman's Dome** (6,643 ft.), highest peak in Tennessee. The visitor should stop first at the Sugarlands Visitor Center, just outside of Gatlinburg.

QUEBEC— THE GASPÉ PENINSULA

This huge land mass is legendary for the seabird colonies of Bonaventure Island. What many have not yet discovered are the marvels of the interior, not least of which is the heartwarming hospitality of the Gaspésiens. Of several outstanding wild areas none surpasses **Gaspésien Provincial Park.** For lushness of flora, variety and richness of wildlife, and relative ease of access it is unrivaled in the Northeast. The trail along the **Sainte Anne River** to the top of **Mount Albert** has yielded boreal owls. Here one may also find the pale Quebec race of the barred owl and the Labrador subspecies of the great horned owl.

NEW BRUNSWICK— GRAND MANAN ISLAND

This beautiful island has long been a favorite of bird finders. It is the southernmost known eastern breeding locality of the boreal owl. Although the author does not know of any recent local nesting records of this much-sought species, the bird is certainly a possibility. Grand Manan, in any case, is one of the few places where a birder may claim to have seen a guillemot and a great horned owl side by side and not be thought insane. Other nesting owl species to be on the alert for here are the long-eared owl and the saw-whet owl.

MAINE

Maine is a mosaic of natural beauty. Three localities are of particular interest because of their vastness, variety, and peripheral amenities.

Moosehorn National Wildlife Refuge, on the outskirts of Calais, is famous for woodcocks, the strange nocturnal sandpiper with eyes on top of its head. People flock to Moosehorn to see the courtship of this bird, locally known as the timberdoodle. At moonrise in March the male timberdoodle flies. Those who gather to see it get a bonus—the bell-like tooting of territorial saw-whet owls. There are many other nightbird finding possibilities in Moosehorn: barred, great horned, and long-eared owls, nighthawks and whippoorwills, and choruses of sora and Virginia rails in the extensive marshes. Diurnal birding and botanizing are superlative.

Baxter State Park, site of Mount Katahdin (5,273 ft.), highest peak in Maine, boasts a diversity of habitats—ranging from marshes, meadows, climax forests of spruce and fir, and open stands of birch and poplar to sphagnum bogs and subalpine krumholtz—and a fauna that is equally varied and includes virtually all the birds of the boreal forest. Great horned, long-eared, barred, and saw-whet owls are regular residents. Hawk and boreal owls are distinct winter possibilities. Both of these species seem to be expanding their range southward. Anyone owling in Baxter in summer should keep an ear peeled for their distinctive love calls.

Acadia National Park is so big, so beautiful, and so exhaustively described in the travel literature that all we need to do here is indicate a few of the species that may delight the owl finder. At night the conifers resound with the booming of barred and great horned owls. Saw-whet owls nest in mixed hardwood-evergreen woodlands in flicker holes. At least once, hawk owls have attempted nesting in the park. Other possibilities: long-eared owls (local nester, winter roosts), short-eared owls (migrant, open fields, marshes), boreal owls (wintering, conifer groves), and snowy owls (winter, open country, shorelines).

NEW HAMPSHIRE

North Conway is a convenient starting point for excursions to **Mount Washington,** hub of northeast alpinism. One may begin the climb at **Pinkham Notch Camp** and take the famous **Tuckerman Ravine Trail** to the summit (6,288 ft.). Or let the car do the climbing. A scenic, well-maintained road will allow your scoobedoo to take you up to the treeline. Either the ascent or the descent will expose you to a multitiered life zone, each layer with its representative species of plants and animals. Saw-whet, great horned, and barred owls can be expected here and in many other areas of the White Mountains. Reports of boreal and hawk owls nesting in northern New Hampshire are dubious, but owlers should be alert for the territorial songs of these species.

MASSACHU-SETTS

Newburyport offers access to **Plum Island** and the **Parker River National Wildlife Refuge.** This legendary birding area is a great spot for snowy owls. In flight years both the island and mainland sections of the refuge afford close views of these magnificent birds. Call the Massachusetts Rare Bird Alert for details. If you come here on a snowy owl safari, don't miss out on the chances of finding a saw-whet owl or two roosting in the dense groves of evergreens scattered throughout the refuge.

If you happen to be one of the countless nature lovers who come to **Cape Cod,** make a stop at the **Wellfleet Bay Wildlife Sanctuary,** a few miles before Provincetown, headquarters for information about natural features and field trips throughout the Cape. Owl finding possibilities include long-eared and great horned owls (year-round), short-eared owls (local nesters, spring and fall migrants), and saw-whet and snowy owls (winter visitants). With a totally straight face ornithologists

have said that bird-watching on **Nantucket** in summertime is a strange experience. Considering the flocks of junior executives that migrate there in July and the antics they engage in the statement is hilarious. Nantucket, nonetheless, is ornithologically unique. As of this writing, it is the last known accessible nesting site in the Northeast of that marvelous acrobat, the short-eared owl. No one who visits Nantucket should miss the courtship of these beautiful birds, which is at its best in early April.

Another famous resort island where summer bird-watching can yield unexpected views is **Martha's Vineyard.** Like Nantucket, the Vineyard has a special owl. The **State Forest,** a rectangular tract of conifers, is notable for its resident population of long-eared owls. Until the late 1970s short-eared owls bred at **Chappaquiddick.** If some of the critical conservation problems in this area are solved, the birds may yet return to this former nesting ground.

NEW YORK

Owl finders in New York have an embarrassment of riches in the vastness of the **Adirondacks.** No one spot can be singled out as excelling over any other for natural riches, including owls. However, the resort of **Lake Placid** is a convenient base for an array of excursions that should include the following highlights: **Chubb River Swamp** is an unsurpassed locality for the characteristic species of the northern coniferous forest. **Whiteface Mountain**'s altitudinal natural layer cake offers possibilities similar to those in Mount Washington, New Hampshire. And don't miss **Marcy Dam, Marcy Lake,** and **Mount Marcy,** the highest peak in the Adirondacks,

just below whose summit is Lake Tear of the Clouds, source of the Hudson River.

There are many other exceptional areas, including the spruce bogs of Madawaska, that the owl seeker should investigate. Tantalizing reports of summering subalpine species like the boreal and hawk owls are worth following up. Excellent information about every aspect of Adirondack exploration and natural history may be obtained at the **Adirondack Mountain Lodge** in Heart Lake, close to Lake Placid. The lodge itself is a fine place to hear great horned owls, barred owls and whippoorwills.

NEW JERSEY

Almost within slingshot distance of New York City are the **Great Swamp National Wildlife Refuge** and coterminous **Summit Nature Center,** over 8,000 acres of hardwood forest, cattail marsh, and lily ponds. In early spring, the three typical eastern owls, screech, great horned, and barred, will often sing together in this enclave of lush wilderness imbedded in the concrete bogs of suburbia.

Cape May, world-famous for fall hawk flights, is a funnel that annually concentrates millions of migrant birds and thousands of migrant bird watchers. Witmer Stone said it all many years ago: "Anything can happen in Old Cape May—and usually does." "Anything" includes late fall flights of barn owls,

saw-whet owls, and long-eared owls, lovingly monitored for years by Katy Duffy and helping hands from the Cape May Bird Observatory. A wide variety of lectures, field trips, and related bird-finding activities are scheduled by this outstanding ornithological institution. Contact the observatory for details on owl programs.

Owl-finding opportunities in the environs of Cape May include saw-whet owls (winter roosts), short-eared owls (marshes along Delaware Bay), and barn owls (nesting in extensive farmlands). **Bellemead State Forest,** just north of Cape May, is a fine spot for screech, barred, and great horned owls.

DELMARVA PENINSULA

Separating Chesapeake Bay from the Atlantic Ocean, Delmarva (*DEL*aware/*MAR*yland/*Virgini*A) is rich in history and wildlife refuges. Three of the latter must be singled out: **Bombay Hook National Wildlife Refuge** (Delaware), **Blackwater National Wildlife Refuge** (Maryland), and **Chincoteague National Wildlife Refuge** (Virginia). These and dozens of other topflight wildlife areas create a nature study area unmatched anywhere on the eastern seaboard. Nightbird finding in Delmarva often combines prowling for nightjars and owls with a sweep of the extensive marshes for rails. Five species of these elusive birds, including the exquisite little black rail, nest in Delmarva. A well-planned Delmarva night run in late spring will regularly yield two nightjars, at least three owls, and no less than four rails.

SOUTH CAROLINA

No combination of wildlife areas is more impressive than that found in the environs of Charleston. The breathtaking beauty of **Bull's Island** in **Cape Romain National Wildlife Refuge** is an irresistible magnet for visiting naturalists. If you are among the many who succumb to Cape Romain, by no means miss looking for barred owls north of Charleston in **Frances Marion National Forest.** This vast wilderness (over 240,000 acres) features extensive cypress-tupelo swamps, mixed hardwood-pine woodlands, and brushy edge areas, with a corresponding wealth of birdlife.

GEORGIA

Okefenokee Swamp and **Okefenokee National Wildlife Refuge,** site of the idyllic Suwannee River, is a great wilderness of marsh and cypress forest encompassing seven hundred square miles of the most romantic fairyland settings for observing the plant and birdlife of the Deep South. Here the barred owl is "King of the Forest." Champion vocalist of the owls, this "Beautiful Screamer" can indeed be heard hard by the Stephen Foster

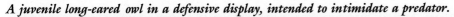

A juvenile long-eared owl in a defensive display, intended to intimidate a predator.

Homestead. Groups of up to thirty owls will sometimes caterwaul together before a thunderstorm. These choruses clearly are the source of the "whangdoodles," the banshees of Dixieland.

Many other avian specialties can be enjoyed in the Okefenokee, notably sandhill cranes, turkeys, and hooded mergansers, a dainty duck of exquisite beauty.

FLORIDA

Kissimee Prairie, extending from just south of Orlando all the way to Lake Okeechobee, is a classic spot for a classic duo of birds: burrowing owls and sandhill cranes. In Florida these birds are year-round residents. However, they are best enjoyed in early spring, when the night air rings with the billy owls' *coo-cooo!* songs and the cranes' leaps are highest. The best sections for owl and crane watching are northwest of Lake Okeechobee.

Corkscrew Swamp Sanctuary, legendary for limpkins and wood storks, makes it possible for you safely and easily to enter a subtropical forest of true magnificence. Gigantic trees at the forest entrance are dwarfed by centuries-old towering cypresses in the interior portions. These are festooned with an incredible variety of air plants. It is a setting worthy of a Black Forest fairy tale by the Brothers Grimm, but with a tropical twist. As a group of birders, usually in a trance, surveys the spectacle—herons and storks feeding young, pileated woodpeckers scooping out rotted limbs at arm's length, parula warblers darting in and out of the Spanish moss, and beneath it all, giant alligators ogling the air for a victim—the odds are high that a brace of

barred owls will be perched on the boardwalk handrail surveying them. For the student of birds of prey Corkscrew holds another attraction: the handsome short-tailed hawk, a great rarity, nests within the refuge.

Like Yellowstone, the Everglades are vast and seldom accurately visualized by the visitor-to-be. Most people who come to **Everglades National Park** for the first time expect to find a tropical lushness that simply isn't there. The "Glades" is essentially a gigantic sea of grass with scattered islands of pines and a few hardwood hummocks. In winter, lured by the warmth and by huge flocks of ibises, spoonbills, and herons, myriad tourists come to the park. If you are one of these, you will be pleased to know that barred owls often haunt the hummocks and have even been known to roost on the Royal Palms close to the Flamingo City Visitor Center. Moreover, the delightful little burrowing owl is a regular winter visitor, often roosting in odd places, such as mangrove tangles. Among the many other exciting features of the park, none is more thrilling than a view of swallow-tailed kites, in the author's opinion the most beautiful bird in the world.

An adult barred owl in Florida's Everglades National Park.

BIBLIOGRAPHY

This bibliography lists titles that have contributed to the substance of the book. The literature on owls is vast and constantly expanding. Readers interested in a comprehensive overview should consult the *Working Bibliography of Owls of the World* (R. J. Clark et al., 1978, National Wildlife Federation). A new edition of this superlative reference is being prepared.

Alcorn, G. D. 1986. *Owls.* New York: Prentice Hall.

Allen, A. A. 1924. A contribution to the life history and economic status of the screech owl (*Otus asio*). *Auk* 41:1–16.

Amadon, D., and J. Bull. 1989. *Hawks and Owls of the World: An Annotated List.* Los Angeles: Western Foundation of Vertebrate Zoology.

American Ornithologists' Union, 1983. *Checklist of North American Birds.* 6th ed. Baltimore.

Armstrong, E. A. 1970. *The Folklore of Birds.* New York: Dover.

Arredondo, O. 1976. The great predatory birds of the Pleistocene of Cuba. *Smithsonian Contributions to Paleobiology* 27:164–187.

Audubon, J. J. 1870. *Birds of America.* Vols. 1 and 2. New York: George R. Lockwood.

Austing, G. R., and J. B. Holt, Jr. 1966. *The World of the Great Horned Owl.* New York: Lippincott.

Balda, R. P., B. C. McKnight, and C. D. Johnson. 1975. Flammulated owl migration in the southwestern United States. *Wilson Bulletin* 87:520–533.

Baldwin, P. H., and J. R. Koplin. 1966. The boreal owl as a Pleistocene relict in Colorado. *Condor* 8:299–300.

Barrowclough, G. F., and S. L. Coats. 1985. The demography and population genetics of owls, with special reference to the conservation of the spotted owl (*Strix occidentalis*). In Gutierrez and Carey, 1985, pp. 74–85.

Bell, G. P. 1979. The owl invasion of Amherst Island, Ontario. *American Birds* 33:245–246.

Bendire, C. 1892. *Life Histories of North American Birds.* Smithsonian Institution, U.S. National Museum, Special Bulletin no. 1. Washington, D.C.

Bent, A. C. 1938 (1961). *Life Histories of North American Birds of Prey, Pt. 2.* New York: Dover.

Bergman, C. A. 1983. Flaming owl of the Ponderosa. *Audubon* November: 66–70.

———. 1985. Invaders from the Far North. *National Wildlife* 23:34–39.

Bildstein, K. L., and M. Ashby. 1975. Short-eared owl robs marsh hawk of prey. *Auk* 92:807–808.

Bonnot, P. 1928. An outlaw barn owl. *Condor* 30:320.

Brewster, W. 1925. The birds of the Lake Umbagog region of Maine. *Bulletin of the Museum of Comparative Zoology* 66 (2):211–402.

Brooks, Maurice. 1965. *The Appalachians.* Boston: Houghton Mifflin.

Bull, E., and M. Henjum. 1987. The neighborly great gray owl. *Natural History* 96:32–41.

Bull, J. 1964. *Birds of the New York Area.* New York: Harper & Row.

———. 1985. *Birds of New York State.* Ithaca, N.Y.: Cornell University Press.

Bunn, D. S., A. B. Warburton, and R. D. S. Wilson. 1982. *The Barn Owl.* Calton, England: T. and A. D. Poyser.

Burton, J. A., ed. 1984. *Owls of the World: Their Evolution, Structure and Ecology.* 2nd ed. Dover, New Hampshire: Tanager Books.

Cameron, A., and P. Parnall. 1971. *The Nightwatchers.* New York: Four Winds.

Carson, R. D. 1962. Courtship behavior of short-eared owl. *Blue Jay* 20:2–3.

Catling, P. M. 1972. A behavioral attitude of saw-whet and boreal owls. *Auk* 89:194–196.

Clark, R. J. 1975. A field study of the short-eared owl, *Asio flammeus* (Pontoppidan), in North America. *Wildlife Monographs* 47:1–67.

———. Distributional status and literature of northern forest owls. In Nero et al., 1987, pp. 47–55.

Clark, R. J., D. G. Smith, and L. H. Kelso. 1978. *Working Bibliography of Owls of the World.* Washington, D.C.: National Wildlife Federation.

Clement, R. 1963. Hawk Owl (*Surnia ulula*). In Todd, 1963.

Coats, S., and P. F. Cannell. 1985. Systematics of the Strigidae. Proceedings of Raptor Research Foundation Symposium, 9–10 Nov., at Sacramento (abstract).

Craighead, F. C., Jr., and D. P. Mindell. 1981. Nesting raptors in western Wyoming, 1947 and 1975. *Journal of Wildlife Management* 45:865–872.

An adult gray owl perches on a branch in a Douglas fir.

Craighead, J. J., and F. C. Craighead, Jr. 1956 (1969). *Hawks, Owls and Wildlife*. New York: Dover.

Cramp, S., ed. 1985. *Handbook of the Birds of Europe, the Middle East, and North Africa: The Birds of the Western Palearctic*. Vol. 4. Oxford: Oxford University Press.

de la Torre, J. 1980. Birds of New Canaan. In *Sketches: A Celebration of Nature in New Canaan*. New Canaan, Conn.: New Canaan Nature Center Association, pp. 25–32.

———. 1983. Talking to owls: tips from a strixine addict. *Connecticut Warbler* 3:7–8.

Dementiev, G. P., et al. 1951. *Birds of the Soviet Union*. Moscow (English language translation, Jerusalem 1966.)

DeSimone, P., M. Root, and D. Roddy. 1985. Barred owl (*Strix varia*) nesting and behavior in northwestern Connecticut. Proceedings of Raptor Research Foundation Symposium, 9–10 Nov., at Sacramento (abstract).

Devereux, J. G., and J. A. Mosher. 1984. Breeding ecology of barred owls in the central Appalachians. *Raptor Research* 18:49–58.

Dice, L. R. 1945. Minimum intensities of illumination under which owls can find dead prey by sight. *American Naturalist* 79:385–416.

Dionne, C. E. 1833. *Les Oiseaux du Canada*. Québec: Université Laval.

———. 1906. *Les Oiseaux de la Province de Québec*. Québec: Dussault & Proux.

DuBois, A. D. 1923. The short-eared owl as a foster-mother. *Auk* 40:383–393.

———. 1924. The nuptial song-flight of the short-eared owl. *Auk* 41:260–263.

Duffy, K. 1985a. Owl banding 1984. *Peregrine Observer* 8:5–6.

———. 1985b. Fall Migration of Barn Owls at Cape May Point, New Jersey. Proceedings of Hawk Migration Conference 4, Hawk Mountain Sanctuary Association, at Rochester, New York, 1986.

———. 1986. Owl banding at Cape May Point 1985. *Peregrine Observer* 9:11–13.

———. 1987. Owls at last! 1986 Cape May Point Owl Banding Project. *Peregrine Observer* 10:19–21.

Duncan, J. R., and P. A. Lane. 1987a. Breeding boreal owls in Roseau County. *Loon* 59:163–165.

———. 1987b. Observations of northern hawk-owls nesting in Roseau County. *Loon* 59:165–174.

Durant, M., and M. Harwood. 1980. *On the Road with John James Audubon*. New York: Dodd, Mead.

Earhart, C. M., and N. K. Johnson. 1970. Size dimorphism and food habits of North American owls. *Condor* 72:251–264.

Eaton, E. H. 1910. *Birds of New York*. Albany: New York State Museum.

Eck, S., and H. Busse. 1973. *Eulen, die rezenten und fossilen Formen*. Die Neue Brehm-Bücherei 469, Wittenberg-Lutherstadt.

Eckert, K. 1979. First boreal owl nesting record south of Canada: a diary. *Loon* 51:20–27.

Ehrlich, P. R., D. S. Dobkin, and D. Wheye. 1988. *The Birder's Handbook: A Field Guide to the Natural History of North American Birds*. New York: Simon and Schuster.

Errington, P. L. 1930. The pellet analysis method of raptor food habits study. *Condor* 32:292–296.

———. 1932a. Food habits of southern Wisconsin raptors. Pt. 1: Owls. *Condor* 34:176–186.

———. 1932b. Studies on the behavior of the great horned owl. *Wilson Bulletin* 44:212–220.

Errington, P. L., F. Hamerstrom, and F. N. Hamerstrom, Jr. 1940. The great horned owl and its prey in north-central United States. *Iowa Agricultural Experimental Station Research Bulletin* 277:758–850.

Evans, D. L. 1980. Multivariate analysis of weather and fall migration of saw-whet owls at Duluth, Minnesota. Master's thesis, North Dakota State University.

———. 1982. Status reports on twelve raptors. U.S. Fish and Wildlife Service Special Report no. 238, pp. 1–68, Washington, D.C.

Everett, M. 1977. *A Natural History of Owls*. London: Hamlyn.

Farrand, J., Jr., ed. 1983. *The Audubon Society Master Guide to Birding*. Vol. 2. New York: Knopf.

Feduccia, A. 1980. *The Age of Birds*. Cambridge: Harvard University Press.

Flieg, G. M. 1971. Tytonidae × Strigidae cross produces fertile eggs. *Auk* 88:178.

Forbes, J. E., and D. W. Warner, 1974. Behavior of a radio-tagged saw-whet owl. *Auk* 91:783–795.

Ford, N. L. 1967. A systematic study of the owls based on comparative osteology. Ph. D. diss., University of Michigan, Ann Arbor.

Forsman, E. 1976. A preliminary investigation of the spotted owl in Oregon. Master's thesis, Oregon State University, Corvallis.

Forsman, E., and E. C. Meslow. 1986. The Spotted Owl. In R. L. Di Silvestro (ed.), Audubon Wildlife Report, National Audubon Society, pp. 743–761, New York.

Forsman, E., E. C. Meslow, and H. M. Wight. 1984. Distribution and biology of the spotted owl in Oregon. *Wildlife Monographs* 87:1–64.

Gelbach, F. R. 1986. Odd couples of suburbia. *Natural History* 95:56–66.

Géroudet, P. 1965. *Les Rapaces Diurnes et Nocturnes d'Europe*. Neuchatel: Delachaux & Niestlé.

Goad, M. S., and R. W. Mannan. 1987. Nest site selection by elf owls in Saguaro National Monument, Arizona. *Condor* 89:659–662.

Godfrey, W. E. 1979. *The Birds of Canada*. Ottawa: National Museums of Canada.

Gould, G. I., Jr. 1974. *The Status of the Spotted Owl in California*. Sacramento: California Department of Fish and Game.

———. 1977. Distribution of the spotted owl in California. *Western Birds* 8:131–146.

———. 1979. Status and management of elf and spotted owls in California. In Schaeffer and Ehlers (1979), pp. 86–97.

———. 1985. Current and future distribution and abundance of spotted owls in California. Proceedings of Raptor Research Foundation Symposium, 9–10 Nov., at Sacramento (abstract).

Gross, A. O. 1927. The snowy owl migration of 1926–27. *Auk* 44:479–493.

———. 1944. Food of the snowy owl. *Auk* 61:1–18.

———. 1948. Cyclic invasions of the snowy owl and the migrations of 1945–1946. *Auk* 64:584–601.

Gutierrez, R. J. 1985. An overview of recent research on the spotted owl. In Gutierrez and Carey (1985), pp. 39–49.

Gutierrez, R. J., and A. B. Carey, eds. 1985. *Ecology and management of the spotted owl in the Pacific Northwest*. U.S. Dept. of Agriculture Forest Service, General Technical Report PNW-185, Washington, D.C.

Gutierrez, R. J., A. B. Carey, and A. B. Franklin, et al. 1985. Juvenile spotted owl dispersal in northwestern California: preliminary results. In Gutierrez and Carey (1985), pp. 60–65.

Hagar, D. C., Jr. 1957. Nesting populations of red-tailed hawks and horned owls in central New York State. *Wilson Bulletin* 69:263–272.

Hamer, T. E., and H. L. Allen. 1985. Continued range expansion of the barred owl (*Strix varia*) in western North America. Proceedings of the Raptor Research Foundation Symposium, Nov. 9–10, at Sacramento (abstract).

Hamer, T. E., F. B. Samson, K. A. O'Halloran, and L. W. Brewer. 1987. Activity patterns and habitat use of barred and spotted owls in northwestern Washington. Presented at Symposium on Ecology and Evolution of Northern Forest Owls, 3–7 Feb., at Winnipeg, Canada.

Harrison, C. J. O., and C. A. Walker. 1975. The Bradycnemidae, a new family of owls from the upper Cretaceous of Romania. *Paleontology* 18:563–570.

Harrison, H. H. 1975. *A Field Guide to Birds' Nests*. Boston: Houghton Mifflin.

———. 1979. *A Field Guide to Western Birds' Nests*. Boston: Houghton Mifflin.

Hayward, G. D., P. H. Hayward, E. O. Garton, and R. Escano. 1987. Revised breeding distribution of the boreal owl in the northern Rocky Mountains. *Condor* 89:431–432.

Heinrich, B. 1987. *One Man's Owl*. Princeton, N.J.: Princeton University Press.

Hosking, E. 1982. *Eric Hosking's Owls*. London: Mermaid Books.

Jacot, E. C. 1931. Notes on the spotted and flammulated screech owls in Arizona. *Condor* 33:8–11.

James, P., and A. Hayse. 1963. Elf owl rediscovered in Lower Rio Grande Delta of Texas. *Wilson Bulletin* 75:179–182.

Johnsgard, P. A. 1988. *North American Owls*. Washington: Smithsonian Institution Press.

Johnson, N. K. 1963. The supposed migratory status of the flammulated owl. *Wilson Bulletin* 75:174–178.

Johnson, R. R., and L. T. Haight. 1985. Status of the ferruginous pygmy-owl in the southwestern United States. Paper presented at 103rd meeting, American Ornithologists' Union, at Tempe, Arizona, Oct. 7–10 (abstract).

Johnson, R. R., L. T. Haight, and J. M. Simpson. 1979. Owl populations and species status in the southwestern states. In Schaeffer and Ehlers (1979), pp. 40–59.

Johnston, R. A. 1956. Predation by short-eared owls on a salicornia salt marsh. *Wilson Bulletin* 68:91–102.

Kerlinger, P., and M. R. Lein. 1986. Differences in winter range among age-sex classes of snowy owls (*Nyctea scandiaca*) in North America. *Ornis scandinavica* 17:1–7.

Kerlinger, P., M. R. Lein, and B. J. Sevick. 1985. Distribution and population fluctuations of wintering snowy owls (*Nyctea scandiaca*) in North America. *Canadian Journal of Zoology* 63:1829–1834.

Knudsen, E. J. 1981. The hearing of the barn owl. *Scientific American* 245:112–125.

Knudsen, E. J., and M. Konishi. 1980. Monaural occlusion shifts receptive-field locations of auditory midbrain units in the owl. *Journal of Neurophysiology* 44:687–695.

Konishi, M. 1973. How the owl tracks its prey. *American Scientist* 61:414–424.

———. 1973. Locatable and nonlocatable acoustic signals for barn owls. *American Naturalist* 107:775–785.

———. 1983. Night owls are good listeners. *Natural History* 92:56–59.

Konishi, M., and A. S. Kenuk. 1975. Discrimination of noise spectra by memory in the barn owl. *Journal of Comparative Physiology* 97:55–58.

La Follette, C. 1983. Bird in Peril [spotted owl]. *Defenders of Wildlife* 57:35.

Ligon, D. J. 1968. *The Biology of the Elf Owl*, Micrathene whitneyi. Misc. Publ., Museum of Zoology, University of Michigan, no. 136. Ann Arbor.

Linblad, J. 1967. *I ugglemarker* [The Owl-watcher]. Stockholm: Bonniers. (Data on vision summarized in Mikkola [1983]).

Linkart, B. D., and R. T. Reynolds. 1985. Breeding biology of nesting flammulated owls (*Otus flammeolus*). Proceedings of Raptor Research Foundation Symposium, 9–10 Nov., at Sacramento (abstract).

Marks, J. S. 1984. Feeding ecology of breeding long-eared owls in southern Idaho. *Canadian Journal of Zoology* 62:1528–1533.

———. 1985. Yearling male long-eared owls breed near natal nest. *Journal of Field Ornithology* 56:181–182.

———. 1986. Nest site characteristics and reproductive success of long-eared owls in southwestern Idaho. *Wilson Bulletin* 98:547–560.

Marshall, J. T., Jr. 1939. Territorial behavior of the flammulated screech owl. *Condor* 41:71–78.

———. 1942. Food and habitat of the spotted owl. *Condor* 44:66–67.

———. 1957. Birds of pine-oak woodland in southern Arizona and adjacent Mexico. Pacific Coast Avifauna, no. 32. Berkeley.

———. 1967. *Parallel variation in North and Middle American screech-owls.* Los Angeles: Western Foundation of Vertebrate Zoology.

———. 1974. S. V. *Strigiformes. New Encyclopedia Britannica* (Macropaedia, vol. 17). Chicago: Encyclopedia Britannica.

Marti, C. D. 1969. Some comparisons of the feeding ecology of four owls in north-central Colorado. *Southwestern Naturalist* 14:163–170.

———. 1974. Feeding ecology of four sympatric owls. *Condor* 76:45–61.

———. 1976. A review of prey selection by the long-eared owl. *Condor* 78:331–336.

———. 1979. Status of owls in Utah. In Schaeffer and Ehlers (1979), pp. 29–35.

Martin, D. J. 1974. Copulatory and vocal behavior of a pair of whiskered owls. *Auk* 91:619–624.

Martin, G. R. 1982. An owl's eyes: schematic optics and visual performance in *Strix aluco. Journal of Comparative Physiology* 145:341–349.

———. 1986. Sensory capacities and the nocturnal habits of owls (Strigiformes). *Ibis* 128:266–277.

März, R., and R. Piechocki. 1976. *Der Uhu.* Neue Brehm-Bücherei 108. Wittenberg-Lutherstadt.

Maslow, J. 1983. *The Owl Papers.* New York: Dutton.

McKeever, K. 1979. *Care and Rehabilitation of Injured Owls.* Rannie, Ontario: The Owl Rehabilitation Research Foundation.

Medlin, F. 1967. *Centuries of Owls.* Norwalk, Conn.: Silvermine.

Mikkola, H. 1976. Owls killing and killed by other owls and raptors in Europe. *British Birds* 69:144–154.

———. 1981. *Der Bartkauz.* Neue Brehm-Bücherei 538. Wittenberg-Lutherstadt.

———. 1983. *Owls of Europe.* Vermillion, S.D.: Buteo Books.

Miller, A. H. 1934. The vocal apparatus of some North American owls. *Condor* 36:204–213.

Miller, L. 1930. The territorial concept in the horned owl. *Condor* 32:290–291.

Mosher, J. A., and C. J. Henny. 1976. Thermal adaptiveness of plumage colors in screech owls. *Auk* 93:614–619.

Mourer-Chauviré, C. 1987. Les Strigiformes des phosphorites du Quercy: systématique, biostratigraphie, et paléobiogéographie. *Documents du Laboratoire de Géologie, Lyon* 99:89–135.

———. 1983. *Minerva antiqua* (Aves, Strigiformes), an owl mistaken for an edentate mammal. *American Museum Novitates* 2773:1–11.

Mowat, F. 1961. *Owls in the Family.* Boston: Little, Brown.

Mumford, R. E., and R. L. Zusi. 1958. Notes on movements, territory, and habitat of wintering saw-whet owls. *Wilson Bulletin* 70:188–191.

Murie, O. J. 1929. Nesting of the snowy owl. *Condor* 31:3–12.

Murphy, C. J., and H. C. Howland. 1983. Owl eyes: accommodation, corneal curvature, and refractive state. *Journal of Comparative Physiology* 151:177–184.

National Geographic Society. 1983. *A Field Guide to the Birds of North America.* Washington, D.C.

Nero, R. W. 1964. Snow owl captures duck. *Blue Jay* 22:54–55.

———. 1980. *The Great Gray Owl, Phantom of the Northern Forest.* Washington, D.C.: Smithsonian Institution Press.

Nero, R. W., H. W. R. Copland, and J. Mezibroski. 1984. The great gray owl in Manitoba, 1968–83. *Blue Jay* 43:130–151.

Nero, R. W., R. J. Clark, R. J. Knapton, and R. H. Hamre. 1987. *Biology and conservation of northern forest owls: Symposium proceeding.* U.S. Dept. of Agriculture Forest Service General Technical Report RM-142, Washington, D.C.

Norberg, R. A. 1968. Physical factors in directional hearing in *Aegolius funereus* (Linné), with special reference to the significance of the asymmetry of the external ears. *Arkiv för Zoologi* 20:181–204.

———. 1970. Hunting techniques of Tengmalm's owl *Aegolius funereus* (L.). *Ornis Scandinavica* 1:51–64.

———. Skull asymmetry, ear structure and function, and auditory localization in Tengmalm's owl *Aegolius funereus* (Linné). *Philosophical Transactions, Royal Society, London, Biological Science* 282(991):315–410.

———. 1987. Evolution, structure, and ecology of northern forest owls. In Nero et al. (1987), pp. 9–43.

Nuttall, T. 1832–1834. *A Manual of the Ornithology of the United States and Canada.* Boston: Hilliard, Gray, & Co.

Palmer, D. A. 1986. Habitat selection, movements and activity of boreal and saw-whet owls. Master's thesis, Colorado State University, Fort Collins.

———. 1987. Annual, seasonal and nightly variation in the calling activity of boreal and northern saw-whet owls. In Nero et al. (1987), pp. 162–168.

Palmer, D. A., and R. A. Ryder. 1984. The first documented breeding of the boreal owl in Colorado. *Condor* 86:215–217.

Payne, R. S. 1962. How the barn owl locates its prey by hearing. *The Living Bird* 1:151–159.

———. 1971. Acoustic location of prey by barn owls (*Tyto alba*). *Journal of Experimental Biology* 56:535–573.

Perrone, M. 1981. Adaptive significance of ear tufts in owls. *Condor* 83:383–384.

Peterson, R. T. 1961. *A Field Guide to the Western Birds*. Boston: Houghton Mifflin.

———. 1980. *A Field Guide to the Birds*. Boston: Houghton Mifflin.

Peterson, R. T., and E. L. Chalif. 1973. *A Field Guide to Mexican Birds*. Boston: Houghton Mifflin.

Pettingill, O. S., Jr. 1977. *A Guide to Bird Finding East of the Mississippi*. New York: Oxford University Press.

———. 1979. *A Guide to Bird Finding West of the Mississippi*. New York: Oxford University Press.

———. 1985. *Ornithology in Laboratory and Field*. New York: Academic Press.

Portenko, L. A. 1972. *Die Schnee-eule*. Neue Brehm-Bücherei 454. Wittenberg-Lutherstadt.

Pough, R. H. 1946. *Audubon Bird Guide: Eastern Land Birds*. New York: Doubleday.

———. *Audubon Bird Guide: Western Birds*. [Owl entries by Joe T. Marshall, Jr.]. New York: Doubleday.

Preble, E. A. 1908. *A Biological Investigation of the Athabaska-McKenzie Region*. USDA Bureau of Biological Survey no. 27. Washington, D.C.

Raptor Research Foundation and University of California, Davis Raptor Center. 1985. Abstracts of papers on biology, status, and management of owls: International Symposium on the Management of Birds of Prey, 9–10 Nov., at Sacramento.

Reynolds, R. T., and B. D. Linkart. 1987a. Fidelity to territory and mate in flammulated owls. In Nero et al. (1987), pp. 239–248.

———. 1987b. The nesting biology of flammulated owls in Colorado. In Nero et al. (1987), pp. 239–248.

Rich, P. V., and D. J. Bohaska. 1976. The world's oldest owl: a new strigiform from the Paleocene of southwestern Colorado. *Smithsonian Contributions to Paleobiology* 27:87–93.

———. 1981. The Ogygoptynigidae, a new family of owls from the Paleocene. *Acheringa* 5:95–102.

Rockwell, R. B., and C. Blickensderfer. 1921. Glimpses of the home life of the saw-whet owl. *Natural History* 21:628–638.

Rome, C. 1980. *An Owl Came to Stay*. New York: Crown.

Ross, A. 1969. Ecological aspects of the food habits of insectivorous screech-owls. *Proceedings of the Western Foundation of Vertebrate Zoology* 1(6):301–344.

Ryder, R. A., D. A. Palmer, and J. J. Rawinski. 1987. Distribution and status of the boreal owl in Colorado. Symposium on Ecology and Evolution of Northern Forest Owls, Feb. 3–7 at Winnipeg, Manitoba.

Santee, R., and W. Granfield. 1939. Behavior of the saw-whet owl on its nesting grounds. *Condor* 41:3–9.

Saunders, A. A. 1913. Some notes on the short-eared owl. *Condor* 15:121–125.

Savage, T. 1965. Recent observations of the saw-whet owl in Great Smoky Mountains National Park. *The Migrant* March: 15–16.

Schaeffer, P., and S. Ehlers, eds. 1979. *Owls of the West: Their Ecology and Conservation*. Tiburon, Calif.: National Audubon Society and Western Education Center.

Service, W. 1969. *Owl*. New York: Knopf.

Seton, E. T. 1911. *The Arctic Prairies*. New York: Scribner's.

Sibley, C. G., and J. E. Ahlquist. 1972. A comparative study of the egg-white proteins of non-passerine birds. *Bulletin of the Peabody Museum of Natural History, Yale University*. 39:1–276.

———. 1986. Reconstructing bird phylogeny by comparing DNA's. *Scientific American* February:82–92.

Silliman, A. J. 1973. Vision. In *Avian Biology*, vol. 3, edited by D. S. Farmer, J. R. King, and K. C. Parkes. New York: Academic Press.

Smith, D. G., and J. R. Murphy. 1973. Breeding ecology of raptorial birds in the eastern Great Basin Desert of Utah. *Brigham Young University, Biological Series* 18:1–76.

Smith, D. G., C. R. Wilson, and H. H. Frost. 1974. History and ecology of a colony of barn owls in Utah. *Condor* 76:131–136.

Smith, D. G., A. Devine, and D. Gendron. 1982. An observation of copulation and allopreening of a pair of whiskered owls. *Journal of Field Ornithology* 53:51–52.

Smith, D. G., and R. Gilbert. 1984. Eastern screech-owl home range and use of suburban habitats in southern Connecticut. *Journal of Field Ornithology* 55:322–329.

Smith, D. G., D. Walsh, and A. Devine. 1987. Censusing eastern screech-owls in southern Connecticut. In Nero et al. (1987), pp. 255–267.

Smith, D. G., and D. H. Ellis. 1988. Raptor status report: snowy owl. Northeast Raptor Management Symposium and Workshop, 16–18 May, at Syracuse.

Sparks, J., and T. Soper. 1970. *Owls: Their Natural and Unnatural History*. Devon, England: David & Charles.

Steadman, D. W. 1981. Review of paleontological papers by C. J. O. Harrison and C. A. Walker. *Auk* 98:205–207.

Steadman, D. W., G. K. Pregill, and S. L. Olson. 1984. Fossil vertebrates from Antigua, Lesser Antilles: evidence for late Holocene human-caused extinctions in the West Indies. *Proceedings of National Academy of Science, U.S.A.* 81:4448–4451.

Stewart, P. A. 1952. Dispersal, breeding behavior and longevity of banded barn owls in North America. *Auk* 69:227–245.

———. 1980. Population trends of barn owls in North America. *American Birds* 34:698–700.

Stillwell, J., and N. Stillwell. 1954. Notes on the call of a ferruginous pygmy owl. *Wilson Bulletin* 66:152.

Stone, W. B. 1988. Causes of morbidity and mortality for, and environmental toxicants in, great horned owls in New York. Final Report, RAGTW (Return a Gift to Wildlife) Project no. W-8, 31 pp., Albany, N.Y.

Stone, W. B., and J. C. Okoniewski. 1983. Organochlorine toxicants in great horned owls from New York, 1981–1982. *Northeast Environmental Science* 2:1–7.

———. 1987. *Organochlorine pesticide-related mortalities of raptors and other birds in New York, 1982–1986*. Department of Environmental Conservation, Wildlife Resources Center, Delmar, New York.

Sutton, G. M. 1927. Ruffed grouse captured by a screech owl. *Wilson Bulletin* 39:171.

———. 1929a. Does the great horned owl have a poor memory? *Wilson Bulletin* 41:247–248.

———. 1929b. Insect-catching tactics of the screech owl (*Otus asio*). *Auk* 46:545–546.

———. 1929c. Notes. [Report of saw-whet owl riding train.] *Cardinal* 2:129–130.

Sutton, G. M., and D. F. Parmelee. 1956. Breeding of the snowy owl in southeastern Baffin Island. *Condor* 58:273–282.

Swainson, W., and J. Richardson. 1832. *Fauna Boreali-Americana. Vol 2, The Birds*. London: J. Murray & Son.

Taverner, P. A., and B. H. Swales. 1911. Notes on the migration of the saw-whet owl. *Auk* 28:329–334.

Taylor, A. L., Jr., and E. Forsman. 1976. Recent range extensions of the barred owl in western North America, including the first records for Oregon. *Condor* 78:560–561.

Taylor, P. S. 1973. Breeding behavior of the snowy owl. *Living Bird* 12:137–154.

Terres, J. K. 1980. *Audubon Society Encyclopedia of North American Birds*. New York: Knopf.

Todd, W. E. C. 1963. *Birds of the Labrador Peninsula and Adjacent Areas*. Toronto: University of Toronto Press.

Townsend, C. W. 1925. Richardson's owl at Grand Manan, New Brunswick. *Auk* 42:131–132.

Tyler, H. A., and D. Phillips. 1978. *Owls by Day and Night*. Happy Camp, California: Naturegraph.

Urner, C. A. 1923. Notes on the short-eared owl. *Auk* 40:30–36.

Van Camp, L. F., and C. J. Henny. 1975. *The Screech Owl: Its Life History and Population Ecology in Northern Ohio*. North American Fauna no. 71. U.S. Dept. of the Interior, Fish and Wildlife Service, Washington, D.C.

Vickery, P. D., and R. P. Yunick. 1979. The 1978–1979 great gray owl incursion across northeastern North America. *American Birds* 33:242–244.

Voous, K. H. 1964. Wood owls of the genera *Strix* and *Ciccaba*. *Zoologische Mededelingen* 39:471–478.

———. 1989. *Owls of the Northern Hemisphere*. Cambridge: MIT Press.

Walker, L. W. 1943. Nocturnal observations of elf owls. *Condor* 45:165–167.

———. 1974. *The Book of Owls*. New York: Knopf.

Watson, A. 1957. The behaviour, breeding and food ecology of the snowy owl, *Nyctea scandiaca*. *Ibis* 99:419–462.

Weinstein, K. 1985. *Owls, Owls—Fantastical Fowls*. New York: Arco.

Wilson, A. 1828. *American Ornithology, or the Natural History of the Birds of the United States*. New York: Collins.

Winter, J. 1979. The status and distribution of the great gray owl and the flammulated owl in California. In Schaeffer and Ehlers (1979), pp. 60–85.

———. 1986. Status, distribution, and ecology of great gray owls in California. Master's thesis, San Francisco State University.

DISCOGRAPHY

The following is a list of commercially available cassettes featuring the calls of North American owls.

Voices of New World Nightbirds: Owls, Nightjars and their Allies. ARA Records, 1986.

A Field Guide to Bird Songs of Eastern and Central North America. Cornell Laboratory of Ornithology. (Accompanies Roger Tory Peterson's *Field Guide to the Birds.*)

A Field Guide to the Songs of Western Birds. Cornell Laboratory of Ornithology. (Accompanies Roger Tory Peterson's *Field Guide to Western Birds.*)

Guide to Bird Sounds. National Geographic Society. (Accompanies the NGS's *Field Guide to the Birds of North America.*)

In addition to these, two excellent identification aids were made available in 1988–1989.

Peterson Bird Guides, Eastern-Central. Birding by Ear: A Guide to Bird Song. Boston: Houghton Mifflin.

Audubon Society's Video Guide to Birds of North America. New York: National Audubon Society. (Volume 3 features the owls.)

INDEX